Newcits – Investing in UCITS Compliant Hedge Funds

For other titles in the Wiley Finance series
please see www.wiley.com/finance

Newcits – Investing in UCITS Compliant Hedge Funds

Edited by Filippo Stefanini

Authors: Tommaso Derossi, Michele Meoli, Silvio Vismara

A John Wiley and Sons, Ltd., Publication

Library of Congress Cataloging-in-Publication Data

Derossi, Tommaso.
  [Fondi Newcits. English]
  Newcits : investing in UCITS compliant hedge funds / Tommaso Derossi, Michele Meoli,
Silvio Vismara ; edited by Filippo Stefanini.
      p. cm.
  "Originally published in Italian I fondi Newcits, c2010 by Il Sole 24 ORE S.p.A."
  "This English language edition translated by Filippo Stefanini."
  Includes bibliographical references and index.
  ISBN 978-0-470-97627-2
  1. Hedge funds–European Union countries.   2. Investments–European Union countries.
I. Meoli, Michele.   II. Vismara, Silvio.   III. Stefanini, Filippo.   IV. Title.
  HG5424.5.D47 2011
  332.64′ 524094–dc22
                                                                            2010044301

A catalogue record for this book is available from the British Library.

ISBN 978-0-470-97627-2 (paperback), ISBN 978-0-470-97949-5 (ebk),
ISBN 978-1-119-99197-7 (ebk), ISBN 978-1-119-99198-4 (ebk)

Set in 11/15pt Times by Aptara, New Delhi, India
Printed in Great Britain by TJ International Ltd, Padstow, Cornwall, UK

Contents

Preface

This book, taking the analysis of the causes of negative investor perceptions of hedge funds as a starting point, elaborates the constraints and the opportunities offered by European directives about UCITS.[1] These allow us to face, and go beyond, the investors' distrust, with the ambition of representing a useful educational tool for the players in such a complex sector. In fact, in Europe, the most important answer to the crisis has been to exploit the principles contained in the UCITS III directive. These principles have guaranteed the solidity of the mutual fund industry during the crisis and have permitted the development of funds managed with investment techniques similar to those used by hedge funds. The UCITS III regulation, with the extension of such principles even to hedge funds, increases the investors' protection and opens to retail investors a world so far perceived as 'elitist', and confined exclusively to high-net-worth individuals or institutional clients. This is of great importance if we consider the wide and growing need of both financial advisory and absolute return products.

A European regulatory framework for alternative asset managers is rapidly evolving. The uncertainty surrounding the directive on Alternative Investment Fund Managers proposed by the European Commission, and the arrival in 2011 of the UCITS IV directive, are strong incentives towards the convergence of an alternative and the

---

[1] Directives 2001/107/CE and 2001/108/CE.

traditional form of asset management. This pushes alternative asset managers to implement some investment strategies into vehicles that are UCITS III compliant. Hedge products that follow the prescriptions of the UCITS III regulation are frequently labelled 'Newcits'. These Newcits funds represent an interesting opportunity to access, with safety, the excellent competencies in the absolute return of those money managers that have been able to navigate the stormy seas of the crisis. According to a recent survey by Hedge Funds Intelligence on 650 investment houses, more than half of the European asset managers have already launched, or are shortly intending to launch, an onshore version of their strategies. In the same direction, another market analysis performed by KDK Asset Management found that about 80% of asset managers have declared their intention to consider a UCITS III compliant version of their hedge funds. The brand UCITS III is therefore perceived positively, despite the fact that some UCITS III funds invested in products linked to Madoff.

We wish to emphasize that if, from one viewpoint, the push of UCITS III compliant hedge funds determines a greater level of protection from operational risks; from another viewpoint there could be an inducement for managers of funds of hedge funds to limit the due diligence activities on money managers and counterparties, compromising the adequacy and the efficacy of the investments. In order to avoid this improper approach, this book can represent a useful support tool. I thank Filippo Stefanini, who has described an exhaustive framework of these new trends that will help all those concerned to make a conscious approach to Newcits funds.

Massimo Mazzini
CEO of Eurizon A.I. SGR and CEO of Eurizon Capital S.A.

Introduction: The Crisis of 2008 and the Way Out

UCITS can be as important to the fund industry as the GSM was for mobile phones. GSM allowed European mobile phone companies to dominate around the world, except for in the US.

Paul Marshall, co-founder of Marshall Wace LLP

The hedge fund industry closed the year 2009 with returns that represent the best result of the last decade. According to our calculations, at the end of 2009, 83% of hedge funds generated positive performances in 2009 and 22% recouped completely the losses of 2008. Hedge Fund Research estimates that at the end of 2009 the hedge fund industry managed $1,600 billion, which was up from $1,400 billion in the previous year, but well below the peak reached in 2007 of $1,868 billion. The number of hedge funds is progressively declining from a peak of 10,096 at the end of 2007, to 9,284 at the end of 2008, and to 9,050 at the end of 2009. Morgan Stanley foresees that at the end of 2010 the hedge fund industry will reach $1,750 billion of assets under management – a level similar to that reached in mid-2007. After the crisis, 2010 appears to be a year during which investors will regain confidence in hedge funds thanks to easier operation, transparency and liquidity than in the past.

At the end of 2008 some critics were laughing: "Do hedge funds still exist?" What happened in September 2008 had no precedent in the history of financial markets and marked the worst month ever in the history of hedge funds. Some interpretations of what happened in that month can help to explain how the hedge fund industry shook under the effect of severe attacks on its foundations.

The first point to consider is the questioning about two pillars of the hedge fund strategies: short selling and leverage. The starting point is represented by the events that happened in September 2008. In the first weekend of September, Fannie Mae and Freddie Mac entered into conservatorship. Lehman Brothers International (Europe) filed for bankruptcy protection on 15 September 2008. With $639 billion of assets, its bankruptcy was six times larger than any other in US history. Furthermore, Lehman had an "investment grade" rating when it failed. This highlighted the fact that the financial leverage used by hedge funds came from brokers where little attention was given to the segregation of client assets from bank assets. Practically, hedge fund assets were often kept in omnibus accounts rather than in non-rehypothecated segregated accounts, and when Lehman Brothers International (Europe) failed, the lack of segregation of assets between hedge funds and prime brokers caused extraordinary financial distress in several hedge funds. In fact, Lehman was the prime broker of several hedge funds and the lack of segregation of assets made it possible for Lehman to rehypothecate the hedge fund assets. Even where Lehman was not the prime broker, they were counterparty to the numerous trades for many hedge funds. In the end, many hedge funds were in a position of unsecured creditors in Lehman's bankruptcy and it became impossible for them to value their portfolios. For this reason, many hedge funds created side pockets, with Lehman claims inside. The reaction of market regulators and politicians to that frightening series of defaults, and to the fall of share prices of financial institutions, was a ban on short selling. That ban made it extremely difficult to work for hedge funds that specialized in *long/short equity*, *equity market neutral*, *convertible bond arbitrage* and *statistical arbitrage* strategies. Those funds, which were used to applying relative value strategies on shares of the financial sector, were forced to limit their exposure to the financial sector.

A second point to consider is the impact of idiosyncratic events on hedge fund performances. We refer in particular to the extraordinarily large short squeeze on Volkswagen shares that occurred in the autumn of 2008. Long before that, many hedge funds had realized that the auto industry would have suffered greatly in that phase of the economic cycle, so they shorted shares of auto producers like Volkswagen. In addition, Lehman was particularly active in borrowing Volkswagen stocks. Suddenly, Porsche announced to the market that it had accumulated a large stake in Volkswagen stocks through derivatives. During the last week of October, the hedge funds that sold short Volkswagen shares were forced to buy back shares in a market with few floating shares. In a joke, Sergio Marchionne, CEO of Fiat, said that Porsche was a hedge fund that also produces cars. On 27 and 28 October, Volkswagen grew to approximately five times its previous value, causing enormous losses to hedge funds that were short that share. BAFIN did not suspend Volkswagen shares for its excessive rise and there were polemics about the lack of transparency in the way Porsche had built its stake in Volkswagen through derivatives. As anticipated, this event – isolated but nevertheless very important – offers an interesting perspective that shows how dangerous short selling can be when risk management procedures are not sufficiently robust.

Another perspective to consider is the role of over-the-counter markets during the crisis, in particular credit default swaps. At the end of 2008 large defaults, both bankruptcies and technical defaults, poured out their effects on the credit default swap market, whose notional value was estimated to be about $45–60 trillion or up to four times the entire US GDP. The outstanding amount of credit default swaps on a single company was uncertain and the tangled web of relationships among counterparties cast dark shadows on the solvency of some large financial institutions. In particular, there were many concerns on the settlement day for technical defaults of credit default swaps for Fannie Mae and Freddie Mac, which caused cash settlements of some $80 billion. The events of technical defaults on credit default swaps on Fannie Mae, Freddie Mac, Lehman, General

Motors and Chrysler tested – for the first time and on such a large scale – this enormous market of over-the-counter derivatives, raising concerns on counterparty risk. Despite all cash settlements having a successful conclusion, the absence of a clearing house to manage counterparty risk was perceived for the first time as being unsustainable. In those days, it seemed clear that such a large market could not be unregulated. Again, the hedge funds were in the eye of the storm as they were one of the main users of credit default swaps. After the policy error of allowing Lehman to fail, the US government was obliged to nationalize AIG because that organization had a huge portfolio of credit default swaps and it was very clear that default by AIG would have had a domino effect on other banks.

An important milestone has been the debate on the transparency of hedge funds. On 11 December 2008, the arrest of Bernard Madoff caused an unprecedented crisis of confidence in hedge funds. Bad press about this $50 billion Ponzi scheme convinced politicians that they could not delay the regulation of the hedge fund industry. Madoff pleaded guilty and was sentenced to 150 years in prison. This is probably the reason for the increased oversight of SEC on hedge fund managers, and the new proposed regulation by the European Commission for offshore funds. Extremely important were the redemptions received by hedge funds and funds of hedge funds at the end of 2008. Around 20% of hedge funds restricted liquidity for their investors because they found an imbalance between the liquidity of the assets in their portfolios and the liquidity they promised to their investors. One hedge fund in five used side pockets, redemption gates, payments in kind, suspension of the calculation of the net asset value (NAV), or often restructured redemptions using very complex legal documentation, which sparked the anger of the redeeming investors and, in particular, of fund of hedge fund managers.

Other core activities of the hedge fund industry were put under discussion. Hedge fund managers often invest a substantial amount of their net worth in the fund they manage in order to provide an alignment of interests with the other investors. In some cases, however, this caused larger liquidity restrictions because the hedge fund managers wanted to continue being investors without paying redemption costs caused by redeeming investors, and without remaining invested in a fund with a higher percentage of illiquid assets. The crisis highlighted the role of proprietary trading desks of large financial institutions, which was very similar to that of large hedge funds. In January 2008, Société Générale announced a record loss of €4.9 billion from its proprietary trading desk.

Another pillar of the hedge fund industry is the high watermark, which is the calculation of performance fees only if the hedge fund exceeds the historical maximum of its NAV. As has been said, this aligns the interests of the fund manager and the investors. Nevertheless, during the crisis many money managers preferred to liquidate the funds that, because of the losses, were too far from the high watermark, otherwise they would have managed the funds for years without earning performance fees. In the second half of 2008, according to Hedge Fund Research, 1,122 hedge funds were liquidated. Too many hedge fund managers chose to liquidate the existing funds and to launch new funds with a new high watermark, showing a moral hazard. This dynamic of asphyxiating launches of new funds can also be explained with higher barriers to entry in the hedge fund industry caused by higher legal costs, compliance costs and internal audit costs to comply with the more stringent regulations.

Another perspective relates to the arrests for insider trading that highlighted the illegal practices of some hedge fund managers.

In this introduction we have shown some interpretations of the financial crisis that have so undermined the foundations of the hedge fund industry that it is impossible for hedge fund managers to continue to do business as usual. Owing to the crisis we are obliged to rethink the strategies of both the hedge fund industry and the fund of hedge funds industry. Nevertheless, hedge funds still exist. A strong need for money management services clearly emerges from the crisis. After all, we are still convinced that hedge fund strategies are very powerful investment tools that allow investment ideas to be expressed in an asymmetric way. Investors are still interested in absolute returns and, at least in perspective, the hedge fund industry has the tools to implement strategies that are able to generate returns that are not too correlated with financial markets. The reaction of hedge fund managers to the crisis has been very different. Some large and well-known hedge funds shut down their activities under the weight of their negative performances. Other hedge fund managers continued to work as usual, thinking that the crisis was not different from past crises. Some others have discussed their operations, creating working groups or best practices to self-regulate themselves but have produced only limited effects. Last, but not least, some others chose the ease, transparency and liquidity offered by the UCITS III directive, which provides a regulatory framework that is well defined and designed to protect the final investor. These money managers found in the existing UCITS III directive a way out from the general lack of confidence that was surrounding the hedge fund industry.

Paul Marshall, founder of the London-based asset manager Marshall Wace LP, compared the UCITS III directive to the GSM standard for mobile phones that has given European mobile phone companies a competitive advantage all over the rest of the world. We believe that the essence of his statement is the role that standardization can have on the asset management industry: ease of operation, liquidity, asset protection, diversification, risk management processes and transparency. Moreover, the UCITS III directive moves the fund domicile from offshore fiscal havens to European countries, fighting against regulatory and tax arbitrage. This directive provides another way out for alternative asset managers and so, in a nice syllogism, pushes hedge fund managers to become mainstream and more and more traditional. The subject of this book is to study this way out in detail, to discuss the possibilities provided, the missed opportunities, and to describe how this new phenomenon is growing. The discussion will follow a top-down view. In the first chapter the UCITS III directive is presented, its contents are discussed and the implications for asset management companies are highlighted. We also mention the evolution of the regulatory framework. In the second chapter, we project the new regulatory requirements on the asset management companies, determining the different business models that money managers can choose if they accept to be compliant with the new regulatory framework. The third chapter is dedicated to the description of the operational models of Newcits. The fourth chapter focuses on hedge-like strategies that can be implemented under the constraints of the UCITS III directive. Finally, the last chapter focuses on Newcits, describing the first steps of this new-born industry in term of characteristics, performances, fee structure and analysis of tracking error in respect to the corresponding offshore funds. Our considerations about the effectiveness of the UCITS III directive and potential developments conclude the book.

1

From UCITS Directive to
UCITS III Provisions

On 20 December 1985, the European Parliament approved Directive 85/611/EEC with the aim of creating a level playing field for the Member States in relation to marketing and management of UCITS (Undertakings for Collective Investment in Transferable Securities) – a class of investment products that includes mutual funds and SICAVs (*société d'investissement à capital variable*, or investment companies with variable capital).

The introduction of this directive, also known as UCITS I, provided a fundamental change: it provided the right, for funds authorized by a Member State, to obtain a so-called European Passport and therefore sell their shares or units also in other European countries.

Although many UCITS I provisions were already entailed in the legal framework of some Member States, the introduction of the passport was considered as the first step towards greater harmonization of the market. According to previous legislation, in fact, no funds could be distributed within the EU without obtaining the necessary permission in each country separately.

On 21 January 2002, two new directives were published with the name UCITS III[1] (2001/107/EC, or "Management Company Directive" and 2001/108/EC, or "Product Directive"). While the UCITS I directive granted the European passport only to those UCIs[2] investing in transferable securities like stocks and bonds, UCITS III extended

---

[1] The second version of the UCITS directive, or UCITS II, contained a number of proposals considered too complex and ambitious and was then abandoned by the European Council of Ministers.

[2] Undertakings for Collective Investments.

this opportunity also to UCIs investing in a much broader range of products, allowing them to increase the set of available strategies.

In the next three sections, we summarize the major innovations introduced by UCITS III and describe the operating model of these new UCITS III-compliant hedge-fund-like products, generally referred to as "Newcits".

1.1   PRODUCT DIRECTIVE

Directive 2001/108/EC, or Product Directive, allows a greater number of UCITS to qualify for the status of "harmonized product" and defines the constraints to be respected in the allocation of assets by the investment vehicle. In addition to securities like stocks and bonds, the directive allows UCITS to make extensive use of derivatives and use them not only with a hedging purpose, but also as a way to achieve higher returns and implement leverage. The use of money market instruments, bank deposits and investment in the shares of other UCIs is permitted. Moreover, it is possible to reproduce indices, although it is still under discussion whether or not the reproduction of hedge fund indices should be allowed.

Table 1.1 shows the constraints faced by UCITS with regard to investment in each class of instrument.

1.2   MANAGEMENT COMPANY DIRECTIVE

The Management Company Directive introduced a set of rules that allows the asset management company to directly offer the administrative and marketing services of UCITS, in addition to traditional fund management activities. Once authorized in a Member State, in fact, a management company can freely exercise its activities in any other Member State, for example through a subsidiary or a branch.

Although Article 5 of the UCITS III directive gives the management company a passport that allows it to exercise in the territory of any Member State for which the activity was authorized, no management company may engage in activities that are different from

Table 1.1   Investment possibilities under UCITS III directive

Asset	Constraints
Money Market Instruments [*Arts. 19(1)A, B, C, H; 22(1), (2)*]	• They are admitted to or dealt in on a regulated market. • They are not traded on a regulated market, but they are issued or guaranteed by a central, regional or local institutions such as central banks, by third countries, by recognized institutions, or by enterprises whose securities are traded on regulated market. • It is not possible for a UCITS to invest more than 5% of its assets in instruments that are issued by a single issuer. Member States may raise the limit up to 10%. However, the total amount of the instruments for which the 5% limit is exceeded cannot represent more than 40% of its assets.
Units of Other Investment Funds [*Arts. 19(1)E; 24; 25(2)*]	• The underlying investment fund has not invested more than 10% of its assets in units of another investment fund. The investment in non-UCITS funds must not exceed 30% of the portfolio. • The level of protection for investors of such funds and the level of supervision on those funds must be equivalent to that established by legislation. The investment in another fund may not exceed 25% of that fund's units.
Deposits with Credit Institutions [*Arts. 19(1)F; 22(1)*]	• They must be repayable on demand or they can be withdrawn. • They are maturing in no more than 12 months. • Less that 20% of the UCITS' assets are held by a same credit institution.

(*continued*)

Table 1.1 Investment possibilities under UCITS III directive (*Continued*)

Asset	Constraints
Financial Derivatives [*Arts. 19(1); 21; 22(1)*]	• The underlying assets consist of instruments covered by the directive, indices, interest rates, exchange rates or currencies, provided that the investment is consistent with the objectives outlined in the fund rules. • The global exposure relating to derivative instruments shall be less than UCITS' NAV. • This exposure is calculated in relation to the current value of the underlying assets, counterparty risk, future market movements and time available to liquidate positions. In the case of OTC derivatives: • Counterparties must be institutions subject to prudential supervision and they must be approved by the competent authorities for UCITS. • Derivatives must be subject to a reliable and verifiable valuation on a daily basis. • They can be sold, liquidated or closed by an offsetting transaction at any time, at their fair value. • Exposure to a single counterparty is less than 5% of UCITS' assets (10% if the counterparty is a bank or a credit institution).
Index-Tracking Funds [*Art. 22a*]	• Less than 20% of the UCITS' assets must be invested in a single issuer (Member States may allow an upper limit of 35% if, according to the objectives of the fund, the goal is the reproduction of an index approved by the competent authorities). • The index must be sufficiently diversified, it must represent an appropriate benchmark and it must be published.

the management of UCITS, unless it is not the additional management of other UCIs not covered by the directive and on which the management company is subject to prudential supervision.

In addition to the management of mutual funds and investment companies, Member States may authorize management companies to provide the following services:

- Management of investment portfolios, including those owned by pension funds. This must happen in accordance with the mandate that was given by investors, if such portfolios include one or more of the securities listed in Section B of ISD (93/22/EEC).
- Advice on investments in securities listed in Section B of ISD (93/22/EEC)

In any case, the authorization of the management company is always subject to the conditions shown in Tables 1.2 and 1.3.

If the type of UCITS provides for the presence of an investment company, this company is subject to the conditions reported in Tables 1.4 and 1.5.

1.2.1   Simplified Prospectus

The Management Company Directive also established, alongside the full version of the prospectus already provided by UCITS I, the publication of a simplified prospectus, in order to make the marketing of products more investor friendly and accessible.

The first part of the simplified prospectus must contain a brief presentation of the UCITS, with information on the date of establishment of the mutual fund or investment company and an indication of the Member State in which the mutual fund or investment company was set up. Also, the following information must be contained in the prospectus:

- Number and type of investment compartments contained in the UCITS;
- Name of the management company, if any;

Table 1.2 Management company: conditions for taking up business

| Minimum Capital Requirements [*Art. 5a (1)A*] | • The management company has an initial capital of at least EUR 125,000.
• When the value of the portfolios of the management company exceeds EUR 250 million, the management company shall be required to provide an additional amount of own funds. This additional amount of own funds shall be equal to 0.02% of the amount by which the value of the portfolios of the management company exceeds EUR 250 million. The required total of the initial capital and the additional amount shall not, however, exceed EUR 10 million.
• Irrespective of the amount of these requirements, the own funds of the management company shall never be less than the amount prescribed in Annex IV of Directive 93/6/EEC.
• Member States may authorize management companies not to provide up to 50% of the additional amount of own funds referred to in the first point if they benefit from a guarantee of the same amount given by a credit institution or an insurance undertaking. The credit institution or insurance undertaking must have its registered office in a Member State, or in a non-Member State provided that it is subject to prudential rules considered by the competent authorities as equivalent to those laid down in Community law. |

(*continued*)

Table 1.2   Management company: conditions for taking up business
(*Continued*)

Location of Head Office and Registered Office *Art. 5a (1)D*]	• Both its head office and its registered office are located in the same Member State.
Directors of Managent Company [*Art. 5a (1)B*]	• They shall possess a good reputation and sufficient experience in relation to the type of UCITS managed by the management company.

Table 1.3   Management company: operating conditions

Organization [*Art. 5f (1)A*]	• The management company must have sound administrative and accounting procedures, control and safeguard arrangements for electronic data processing and adequate internal control procedures.
Conflict of Interests [*Art. 5f (2)*]	• The management company shall not be permitted to invest all or a part of the investor's portfolio in units of unit trusts/common funds or of investment companies it manages, unless it receives prior general approval from the client.
Delegation of Own Functions to Third Parties [*Art. 5g(1) A, E, I, (2)*]	• Member States may allow management companies to delegate the exercise on behalf of one or more of their functions provided that the competent authorities are informed. • A mandate with regard to the core function of investment management shall not be given to the depositary or to any other undertaking whose interests may conflict with those of the management company or the unit holders. • The UCITS' prospectuses list the functions that the management company has been permitted to delegate.

Table 1.4 Investment company: conditions for taking up business

Minimum Capital Requirements [*Art. 13a (1)*]	• If the investment company has not designated a management company (i.e. it is "self-managed", the initial capital must be at least EUR 300,000.
Legal Form [*Art. 12*]	• The Member States shall determine the legal form that an investment company must take.
Directors of Management Company [*Art. 13a (1)*]	• They must meet the requirements of a good reputation and they must be sufficiently experienced in relation to the type of business carried out by the investment company.

- Expiration date of the UCITS, if any;
- Custodian bank;
- Auditors;
- Promoters of the UCITS.

The second part of the simplified prospectus provides investment information, indicating the objectives and policies of the investment company or investment fund, as well as a brief assessment of risk profiles. In this section it is also required to present the historical

Table 1.5 Investment company: operating conditions

Organization [*Art. 13c*]	• An investment company must have sound administrative and accounting procedures, control and safeguard arrangements for electronic data processing and adequate internal control procedures.
Management on Behalf of Third Parties [*Art. 13b*]	• Investment companies may only manage the activities of their portfolios and cannot, in any circumstances, receive any mandate to manage assets on behalf of third parties.

performance of the mutual fund or investment company (with the caveat that this is not an indicator of future performance) and the profile of the typical investor for whom the fund or the investment company is designed.

The third part contains information about taxation, entry and exit fees and any other costs, distinguishing between those charged directly to unit holders and those to be charged to the fund or investment company.

The following section includes commercial information, such as how to purchase and sell shares, how to move from one compartment to another with the amount of fees to be paid (when the UCITS is split into several compartments), the date of distribution of dividends, as well as the timing, place and way in which prices are published.

Finally, the investor should be informed about the opportunity to get, at no cost and at any time, a copy of the full prospectus. This last section must also indicate the competent authority, the contacts from whom to receive more information and the date of publication of the prospectus.

1.3   ADDITIONAL REGULATORY LIMITS IMPOSED BY UCITS III

1.3.1   The Prohibition on Borrowing and Short Selling

In addition to the general requirements and limitations that apply to a UCITS, there is the prohibition on borrowing as a means to implement leverage. Article 36 of the UCITS III directive, in fact, clearly states that neither the investment company nor the custodian bank (on behalf of mutual funds) are authorized to borrow money, with the exception of the purchase of foreign currencies by means of "back-to-back"[3] loans. Notwithstanding this prohibition, provided that the loans are just temporary, Member States may authorize UCITS to

---

[3] "Back-to-back" are loans where two companies that are located in different countries lend each other a certain amount of money in their respective currencies (at spot exchange rate) and then return it to one another at maturity.

borrow an amount that is equal to 10% of their assets (in the case of an investment company) or 10% of the value of the fund.

Investment companies can also borrow up to 10% of their assets if these loans are aimed at the purchase of immovable property (i.e. buildings, offices, etc.) that is essential for the direct pursuit of its business. In any case, the amount of these loans, together with temporary loans, may not exceed 15% of their assets, if summed to the temporary ones.

Even if repurchase agreements (or repos) are not permitted, the fund may still leverage up to a maximum of 200% of NAV using derivatives such as futures, swaps or CFDs.

Finally, Article 42 states that neither the investment company, nor the management company, nor the depositary (on behalf of mutual fund) may carry out uncovered sales of transferable securities, money market instruments or other financial instruments referred to in Article 19(1)(e), (g) and (h).

Later in this book, we will present the main strategies adopted by Newcits fund managers and will show how it is possible to overcome these limitations by taking synthetic positions using so-called Contracts for Difference, or CFDs.

1.3.2   Prohibition on Investment in Commodities

Directive 85/611/EEC [Art. 19(2)d] specifies that a UCITS may not acquire precious metals or certificates representing them. In general, the use of commodity derivatives is also not permitted, even though on this point there are still different interpretations of the directive in relation to their eligibility.

However, the prevailing interpretation is that the use of structured products, even when the underlying instruments are not allowed by the UCITS III provisions (oil and other raw materials, for instance) is allowed, provided that these products qualify as "transferable" (i.e. they are sufficiently liquid, marketable and market prices are always available and reliable).

CESR considers that indices based on financial derivatives on commodities are eligible.

1.4 THE NEXT STEP: UCITS IV DIRECTIVE AND NEW PROVISIONS BY EU

On 13 January 2009, the European Parliament approved Directive 2009/65, or UCITS IV, which reforms various aspects of Community law in relation to UCITS. Member States are expected to adopt this set of provisions starting from 1 July 2011. One of the most important aspects of the directive is the introduction of a "management passport" that will make it possible for an investment company to be managed by a management company established in another Member State, if certain requirements are met.

With this new definition of passport, a manager who wishes to replicate one of his products in another Member State would no longer need to create a replica of the fund, but could sell the same product abroad, with the only requirement that the custodian bank is placed in the host country. In this case, the directive provides that the management company is subject to the supervision of the Member State of origin, while the investment company should observe the rules of the Member State in which the UCITS is managed.

Another major innovation is the harmonization of procedures for cross-border mergers of funds, which reduces the administrative burden on management companies.

The directive introduces new rules on master–feeder structures, which allow a UCITS called a "feeder" to invest all or part of its assets in another UCITS called a "master". This provision is expected to foster the development of new business opportunities and to increase the efficiency of investment policies.

Finally, the provisions of UCITS IV will have a significant effect on the delivery of information to investors. The simplified prospectus will be replaced by a so-called "Key Investor Information" (KII), or more probably from a "Key Investor Document"[4] (KID), which is a simple statement of one page that contains information that is essential to assess the investment in the UCITS. The aim of the KID

---

[4] This terminology is considered most appropriate as it emphasizes the need to create a document that has a standardized format for all UCITS and makes comparison between products easier.

is also to compare different investment opportunities more easily, especially in terms of costs and risk profile.

While these provisions have been welcomed by most of the states involved, Luxembourg and Ireland (where the majority of UCITSs are managed) have shown several doubts. The two countries, fearing to lose their hegemony as Member States of origin, said they were reluctant to maintain vigilance on funds that are domiciled elsewhere and do not have any actual presence in the nation. Another concern of the authorities of both countries is the lack of control over accounting and pricing.

However, the introduction of the European passport would avoid the creation of clones and pave the way for cross-border mergers, while the increase in assets under management would create economies of scale and reduce both organizational and management costs. According to some estimates,[5] in Europe, there are over 36 000 funds, compared to the 8000 US funds; in both cases, assets under management are about 5 trillion dollars in total. It is clear that UCITS IV is therefore an important opportunity to increase organizational efficiency and rationalize procedures. Cross-border mergers will not necessarily lead to the loss of supremacy and supervision of Dublin or Luxembourg. If mergers will allow funds to be raised from different sources in a single structure, in fact, companies will be more inclined to choose well-functioning international jurisdictions in which to establish their funds, like Ireland or Luxembourg. Thus, the two countries could still maintain their leading position as States of origin of funds through the supervision of the management company.

In summary, the main innovations introduced in the UCITS IV directive are the following:

- simplification of the notification procedure;
- replacement of the simplified prospectus with the *Key Investor Document* (KID);

---

[5] *Ignites*, the online magazine of Financial Times

- management company passport;
- master–feeder structures;
- mergers between UCITSs.

1.5 SIMPLIFICATION OF THE NOTIFICATION PROCEDURE

UCITS III provides previous notification to the competent authority of the host country, followed by continuous interaction with the same authority during all the subsequent stages. Before the fund may be marketed, it is also necessary to have a waiting period of 2 months and a translation of all the required documents.

Several measures have already been adopted in order to simplify and speed up this process. For example, in June 2006, CESR had published guidelines on simplification of the notification procedure of foreign harmonized UCITSs, while, the following year, the European Commission had announced some details regarding the powers of the Member State of origin and host Member States in the marketing of UCITSs.

The UCITS IV directive will provide interaction between the competent authorities of the country of origin and the host country, only requiring that the KID is translated into the language of the host country. The waiting period will also drop from 2 months to 10 days and the competent authority of the host country will carry out ex-post controls.

1.6 REPLACEMENT OF THE SIMPLIFIED PROSPECTUS WITH THE KEY INVESTOR DOCUMENT

The simplified prospectus provided by UCITS III has the function of presenting basic information about the UCITS that is subject to underwriting, in order to give the investor the possibility to make an aware decision. However, so far, this document does not seem to have achieved its goals, as it was probably considered too long and complex by the average investor, as well as inappropriate to allow easy comparison between different UCITS.

For this reason, the new document provided by the UCITS IV should only contain:

- a brief description of the objectives and the investment policy of the UCITS;
- the presentation of past performance;
- fees and costs connected with the investment;
- the risk/return profile of the investment, including appropriate guidelines and warnings about the other possible risks.

This information shall be written in a concise and non-technical language.

In the document published on 8 July 2009, CESR gave its opinion on the complete and detailed content of KID, also providing:

- specific requirements in the case of umbrella (or multi-compartment) UCITS, funds of funds, master-feeder structures, structured UCITS, UCITS with capital protected, etc.;
- specific details of format and presentation of the KID;
- specific conditions for the provision of key investor information.

The main consequences of this legislation include:

- regulation for issuers: a new simplified prospectus scheme has entered into force that anticipates some form and content of the KID;
- how to communicate so-called "local information" (i.e. information on how to buy or sell): the use of signposting (the publication on a website) was preferred over direct inclusion in the KID, in order to make the document easier to read.

1.7   MANAGEMENT COMPANY PASSPORT

The management passport granted by UCITS III is just "partial", as it allows both asset management on behalf of third parties and distribution of funds but it still does not permit to establish mutual funds in Member States other than their country of origin.

By contrast, UCITS IV will recognize this possibility, thus abandoning the principle of the UCITS home Member State uniqueness, which currently requires that the manager, the product and the custodian bank be placed in the same country.

However, the custodian bank will have to be located in the UCITS home Member State under the shared supervision and responsibility of the authorities "home" and "host".

In the document published on 8 July 2009, CESR gave its opinion on the following issues:

- organizational requirements and conflicts of interest in the management company;
- rules of conduct and conflict of interest in the management company;
- risk management;
- obligations of the depositary;
- control procedures and investigation by the competent authorities
- procedures for exchange of information between the competent authorities;
- application of the rules of conduct, which are prepared by the State of origin of the branch.

1.8   MASTER–FEEDER STRUCTURES

The limitations imposed by UCITS III prevent a mutual fund to invest its entire capital in one another fund. Consequently, mutual funds are not currently allowed to set up harmonized "master–feeder structures" (where the function of the feeder funds is to raise capital that is then invested in one another fund, called "master").

Under the new UCITS IV rules, a feeder fund will be able to invest at least 85% of its assets in one master fund, while the remaining 15% will be invested in other assets such as cash, securities, or immovable assets.

The following rules are also defined:

- The feeder funds may be established in Member States other than the master fund;
- A master cannot itself be a feeder and cannot invest in a feeder. At least one UCITS feeder fund must be present among the unit-holders of the master.

In the document published on 8 July 2009, CESR gave its opinion in terms of master-feeder structures:

- agreement between master and feeder and rules of conduct (if the master and the feeder are operated by the same company);
- measures to prevent "market timing" (coordination of master and feeder in the calculation of NAV);
- settlement, merger and split of a master;
- agreement between the custodians of the master and the feeder (if different);
- reporting requirements by the depositary of the master;
- agreement between the auditors of the master and the feeder (if different).

The law here seems to present some critical issues that are still unresolved, for instance in relation to:

- Which law is applicable to the agreement between master and feeder: the law of the State of origin of the feeder, of the master, of a third country, or leave the choice to the UCITS;
- the type of irregularities that are believed to have a negative impact on the feeder UCITS;
- the role of the custodian of the feeder and the master.

1.9 MERGERS BETWEEN UCITS

This section of the UCITS IV directive sets the rules for mergers involving two or more UCITS or UCITS compartments.

Since the UCITS involved in the merger may be formed in different forms (contractual, corporate or unit trust), mergers could take place between an investment company and a mutual fund (see Art. 38, subpar.1). The provisions of the directive on mergers that refer to UCITS also include their compartments (Art. 37, subpar. 2).

Although some Member States can only authorize contractual funds, these rules do not require Member States to introduce new legal forms of UCITS, because each Member State will have to allow and recognize cross-border mergers between all types of funds (see Art. 26).

Scope

Mergers falling within the scope of the directive may be (see Art. 38, subpar. 2):

- **Cross-border:** mergers between UCITS (including at least two established in different Member States) or mergers between UCITS established in the same Member State in a newly created UCITS established in another Member State.
- **National:** mergers between UCITS established in the same Member State, where at least one of the involved UCITS has been authorized to the cross-border marketing (in accordance with Art. 93). This means that mergers between UCITS that are established in the same Member State and that did not conduct the notification procedure for cross-border marketing fall outside the scope of the directive (but they are still subject to national rules).

General Principles

The directive refers to the three most common techniques of merger that are used in the Member States:

- Incorporation merger;
- Classical merger;
- Merger following partial transfer.

This does not imply an obligation for all Member States to include all of the three techniques in their national law. However, each

Member State must approve the transfer of assets developing from these merger techniques (see par.28).

The new directive also does not prevent the use of other merger techniques on a national level when none of the UCITS involved in the merger has been authorized to the cross-border marketing of its units. These mergers are subject to the relevant provisions of national law (see par.28.)

Incorporation Merger

A merger is a financial operation where one or more UCITS transfer all their assets and liabilities to another existing UCITS (recipient) in exchange for the allocation of units of the recipient UCITS (and, if applicable, a cash payment not exceeding 10% of net asset value of such units) to the holders of the merging funds (Art. 37, *letter a*). *After the merger has become effective, the merging UCITS shall cease to exist.*

Classical Merger

A classical merger is a transaction where two or more UCITS transfer all their assets and liabilities to a new UCITS (recipient) created by them, in exchange for the allocation of units of the recipient UCITS (and, if applicable, a cash payment not exceeding 10% of net asset value of such units) to the holders of the merging funds (Art. 37, letter b). After the merger has become effective, the merging UCITS shall cease to exist.

Merger Following Partial Transfer

A merger with partial transfer is a transaction where one or more merging UCITS transfer all their equity to an existing UCITS or to a new UCITS created by them (recipient).

In this case, the net assets of the merging UCITS shall be transferred to the recipient or, if necessary, to the depositary of the recipient. In addition, the merging UCITS continue to exist until all liabilities have been settled.

Applicable Law

The techniques used for cross-border mergers should be included under the law of the UCITS home Member State, while domestic mergers falling within the scope of the directive must be included under the existing provisions of the Member State in which the merging UCITS are established.

Authorization Procedure for Merger: General Principles

Mergers falling within the scope of the directive are subject to prior authorization by the authorities of the home Member State of the merging UCITS. When merging UCITS are established in different Member States, the competent authorities of each State must work closely together through an appropriate exchange of information before approving the merger. In addition, also the interests of the unit-holders of the recipient UCITS have to be considered by the authorities of its home state.

Checks Undertaken: Custodians and Auditors

Both custodians of merging and recipient UCITS must carry out a series of controls. They should verify the compliance with the requirements of the directive, with the rules of the fund, with the acts constituting the type of merger, with the type of UCITS involved, with the date of effectiveness of the merger and with the rules that apply to the transfer of assets and exchange of shares.

A custodian or a qualified independent auditor[6] (pursuant to Directive 2006/43/EC) shall prepare a report on behalf of all investment funds affected by the merger in order to explicate:

- the criteria used for evaluation of assets and liabilities at the date on which the merger takes effect;

---

[6] With the term "independent auditors" are meant the statutory auditor of the merging UCITS and the statutory auditor of the recipient UCITS.

- the payment in cash per share or unit (if any);
- the method adopted for the calculation of the exchange ratio;
- the actual exchange ratio set at the date on which the merger takes effect.

In order to limit the costs associated with cross-border mergers, it should be possible to compile a single report for all UCITS involved.

Information for Unit-Holders of Merging and Recipient UCITS

Both the merging and the recipient UCITS must provide adequate and accurate information on the transaction to their respective participants, so that they can assess the impact of the proposal on their investment.

This information should include:

- the motivation for the merger proposal;
- the possible impact of participants, including any differences in policies, investment strategies, costs, expected returns, reporting and taxation;
  o any specific right that participants have in relation to the merger proposed. This includes the right to obtain additional information, the right to request a copy of the report of the independent auditor or the depositary, the right to require the repurchase or redemption or, if appropriate, the conversion of its units/shares to regulatory requirements;
- the procedural aspects and the date on which the merger becomes effective;
- a copy of essential information (KII) about the recipient UCITS.

This information is provided to participants of the UCITS involved only after the authorities of the State of origin of the merging UCITS have authorized the operation, but at least 30 days before the deadline for the repurchase or redemption or, if appropriate, the conversion of the units/shares.

If the merging or the recipient UCITS has been authorized to the cross-border marketing, such information must be provided in the official language or one of the official languages of the host State, or in a language approved by the respective competent authorities.

Approval of the Merger by the Participants

If the legal framework of a Member State requires the approval by the participants of the UCITS affected by the merger, such approval may not require more than 75% of the votes actually cast by the participants or represented at the general meeting of the participants.

This provision does not affect the quorum prescribed by national law, but where appropriate, Member States shall not impose a quorum that is more stringent than that applicable to domestic mergers. In addition, they may not require a quorum that is more stringent than those contained in the provisions for mergers of corporate entities.

Rights of Participants of Merging and Recipient UCITS

Under Article 45, par.1 of the directive, the participants of both the merging and the recipient UCITS have the right to request at no cost (with the exception of those held by the UCITS for divestiture, as indicated in their prospectuses. See Art. 30):

- the repurchase or redemption of their units/shares;
- where possible, the conversion of their units/shares in units/shares of another UCITS with similar investment policies and managed by the same management company or any other company with which the management company is linked by common management or control or by a substantial direct or indirect participation;

This right shall take effect as soon as all the participants are informed about the merger and it should end five days prior to the date of calculation of the exchange ratio.

Notwithstanding Article 84, par.1 of the Directive (under which a UCITS repurchases or redeems its units at the request of the holder of units/shares), Member States may allow their competent authorities to require or authorize the temporary suspension of the subscription, repurchase or redemption of units/shares, provided that the aim of such suspension is the protection of the participants (see Art. 45, subpar. 2).

Any legal, consulting or administrative fees related to the preparation and completion of the merger cannot be borne by merging or recipient UCITS or by participants. This rule does not apply when the UCITS have not designated a management company (for example in the case of a self-managed SICAV).

1.10 NEW EU DIRECTIVE ON ALTERNATIVE INVESTMENTS

The crisis that hit markets in the second half of 2007 drew attention to several weaknesses in the financial system and called for an overhaul of supervisory arrangements and regulations involving all the major players in European financial markets.

On 30 April 2009, the European Commission published a draft law concerning the alternative investment market that is pushing management companies specialized in hedge funds to rethink their offer by introducing UCITS III-compliant products. If both the European Council (ECOFIN) and the European Parliament will find an agreement on the text of the directive, the new rules are expected to come into force in 2011. But what are the contents of the proposal?

The main objective of this directive is the introduction of a new framework at European level that is effective and "harmonized", in order to allow the regulation of AIFM (Alternative Investment Fund Managers), which include undertakings for collective investment such as hedge funds, private equity funds, real estate funds and commodity funds. The term "alternative" includes all those funds that do not currently classify as "harmonized" under the UCITS directive.

The main objectives of the AIFM directive are the following:

- ensure that all AIF operators comply with the requirements of appropriate licensing and registration;

- provide a framework for better control of so-called "macro-prudential" risk, for example through the sharing of relevant information between supervisors;
- improve risk management and organizational precautions to reduce the micro-prudential risks;
- increase the level of shareholder protection;
- increase the level of transparency for AIF owning controlling stakes in companies;
- develop a single market for alternative investment funds.

Through the application of these principles, the AIFM directive aims to limit some important classes of risk (see Table 1.6), with the purpose to protect not only the interests of investors, but also the interests of other stakeholders such as creditors, counterparts and the entire European financial market.

It has to be noticed that the nature and intensity of these risks may vary substantially depending on the business model pursued by operators. For example, the so-called "macro-prudential risks" associated with the use of leverage mainly concern the activities of hedge fund managers and commodity funds, while the risks associated with the management of the companies included in the portfolio mainly relates to Private Equity funds.

Other risks, such as those related to the management of "micro-prudential risks" (for instance internal risk management systems) and investor protection are common to all types of AIF.

Many of these risks have actually occurred recently and they have been the primary cause of many upheavals in financial markets. For example, the sudden settlement of large leveraged positions by hedge funds in response to tightening credit conditions, as well as investor redemption requests had a significant role in the collapse of the market and considerably reduced the level of liquidity.

Given the global nature of their activities, many of the risks associated with AIF do have an international dimension and their consequences might be felt beyond national borders. This explains the

Table 1.6 Overview of the main risks. *Source:* Commission of European Communities.

	Source of risk
Macro-prudential (systemic) risks, in particular the use of leverage	• Direct exposure of systemically important banks to the AIFM sector • Pro-cyclical impact of herding, risk of concentration in particular market segments and deleveraging on the liquidity and stability of financial markets
Micro-prudential risks	• Weakness in internal risk management systems with respect to market risk, counterparty risks, funding liquidity risks and operational risks
Investor protection	• Inadequate investor disclosures on investment policy, risk management, internal processes • Conflicts of interest and failures in fund governance, in particular with respect to remuneration, valuation and administration
Market efficiency and integrity	• Impact of dynamic trading and short selling techniques on market functioning • Potential for market abuse in connection with certain techniques, for example short-selling
Impact on market for corporate control	• Lack of transparency when building stakes in listed companies (e.g. through use of stock borrowing, contracts for difference), or concerted action in 'activist' strategies
Impact on companies controlled by AIFM	• Potential for misalignment of incentives in management of portfolio companies, in particular in relation to the use of debt financing • Lack of transparency and public scrutiny of companies subject to buy-outs

need to establish uniform criteria to maintain a proper level of market stability.

What are, in detail, the main provisions introduced by the directive, and how are they going to be applied?

First, all AIFMs domiciled in Europe with more than 100 million euro[7] in assets under management will have to be approved by the competent authorities of the Member State and will be obliged to meet a series of requirements.

Second, all AIFMs operating within the European Union will have to prove to be sufficiently qualified to offer their investment services. They will have to provide adequate and detailed information about the planning of their activities, the identity and profile of managers, the governance of the fund, the risk management measures adopted in the custody of their assets and the methods of reporting. The AIFM will also hold a minimum level of cash as collateral.

In reference to the methods of reporting, more stringent requirements will be introduced that will oblige AIFMs to provide periodic information about markets and instruments where the capital is invested, in addition to performance data and risk concentration.

If compliant with these requirements, an AIF authorized by a Member State will be allowed to market its shares or units in another Member State using a simple notification procedure that consists in the transmission of relevant information from one country to another.

In addition to general requirements, there are some provisions that would only concern alternative investment fund managers engaged in specific activities. These provisions take account of differences in business models of operators and they adapt more easily to their risks.

For instance, operators that make extensive use of leverage would be required to provide additional information to investors and they should inform the competent authorities about their actual leverage. Moreover, in case of AIFM buying shares in companies, additional

---

[7] The threshold is set to 500 million euros in the case of AIFM without leverage and a lock-in provision of at least 5 years.

information requirements would apply when a controlling stake is reached.

Finally, the requirements contained within the proposal as a whole would impose additional administrative burdens to operators, but their size is still uncertain and in any case, they would mainly depend on the existing national requirements in the country of origin.

Thus, the eventual approval of this draft law poses a series of doubts and concerns for alternative investment fund managers, with the effect of further encouraging management companies specialized in hedge funds to revise their offer drastically by introducing harmonized UCITS III products.

2

Business Models for the Production of Newcits and Managed Accounts

The need for access to hedge funds in a way that limits the operational risks and, at the same time, gives greater liquidity and transparency has long been felt by many large institutional investors. Until yesterday, the only alternative to direct investment in hedge funds was the creation of a "managed account", managed by an alternative asset management company. In this section, we compare the managed account with the new business model proposed by Newcits funds, (i.e. those hedge-fund-like products that respect the rules established by the UCITS III directive).

In brief, managed accounts are tailor-made solutions where the operational framework is completely defined by the investor and where the role of the alternative asset manager is limited to pick the securities and to send buy/sell orders. Managed accounts often have the legal form of an offshore investment fund that is managed in parallel with the "flagship fund" that the manager wants to replicate.

The development of managed accounts started in the late Nineties. These platforms were born with the purpose to distribute structured products that give the possibility to invest in hedge funds, offering customers the capital guarantee through portfolio insurance techniques like "Constant Proportion Portfolio Insurance" (CPPI). Today, managed accounts are also used by funds of hedge funds to invest in a liquid and transparent way, without the need to conduct a due diligence on each hedge fund separately, but rather only once, on the entire platform.

So far, managed accounts require an additional complexity at front office and middle office level for the asset managers and for this reason they often accept these tailor-made solutions only for minimum sizes that range from $20 to $50 million. Only the largest institutional investors can afford these minimum investment requirements.

Especially among funds of funds, the solution of platforms of managed accounts is more widespread.

Currently, the largest managed account platforms are Lyxor of Société Générale, Innocap of BNP Paribas, CASAMAR of Crédit Agricole, HFR, Deutsche Bank and Man Investments. In 2009, Infovest21 found about 20 platforms that managed between $30 billion and $50 billion and it estimates that over the next 3–5 years managed accounts platforms will represent about 15–20% of all assets invested in hedge funds, an increase of 2–4% in respect to the end of 2009.

Managers of these platforms select their favourite hedge fund managers, they make a careful due diligence on them and then they open a managed account where the hedge fund manager is a trading advisor whose only duty is to send buy/sell orders on behalf of the managed account. The companies that created the first platforms of managed accounts have identified an operational framework that provides independent valuation, independent asset custody, middle and back office services, an overlay of additional monitoring and risk management, standardized legal set-up and reporting to clients that offers standardized transparency.

Most managed accounts platforms are characterized by better liquidity terms than the corresponding hedge funds. Moreover, managed accounts offer an independent valuation of the portfolio, segregation of assets to prevent fraud and risk management services to avoid a possible manager style drift. The main limitations of these platforms are the additional costs bear by investors, the tracking error between the performance of the flagship fund and the managed account and the fact that they are offshore funds that are directed almost exclusively to institutional investors.

We now focus on the UCITS III-compliant hedge-like products, or Newcits, which also offer a high level of protection for the investor and provide simplicity, transparency and liquidity. In addition, the compliance with UCITS III offers a greater level of standardization. First, it is interesting to note that Newcits could potentially eliminate a level of intermediation in respect to managed account platforms. Indeed, in those cases where the Newcits is present, it has a cost structure that is cheaper than the managed account platform, as managed accounts have an additional layer of fees.

Some of the most popular hedge fund managers have recently launched Newcits. Among these, we report Brevan Howard Asset Management, GLG Partners and Odey Asset Management. At the same time, also some of the most important mutual funds managers have launched this type of product: Blackrock, Gartmore, Cazenove and HSBC. Indeed, in 2009, the French management company Exane has converted its entire product portfolio in UCITS III-compliant products. Even some large investment banks have decided to create platforms with the purpose to offer UCITS III-compliant products: Merrill Lynch, DB Platinum, Schroeders GAIA, GAM Star, etc. These are not managed account platforms, but platforms of UCITS III funds. Within each platform, the level of standardization is even higher because each platform is indeed an investment company with an umbrella structure made up of several Newcits.

Investment banks select the best management companies for their clients, they offer monitoring and risk management services and they leave companies free to work with the counterparts they prefer. In some cases, Newcits are synthetic products that only contain a total return swap issued by the investment bank with the aim of giving investors the performance of an underlying hedge fund: of course, the complexity and the risks of products like these are very high.

A very important aspect is that Newcits platforms offer marketing and distribution services to alternative management companies. The aim of these investment banks is to add many other funds to their umbrella investment companies, giving management mandates to those they assess are the best hedge fund management companies. For example, Merrill Lynch Investment Solutions aims to have about

15 active funds by the end of 2010 with more than 2 billion dollars of assets under management.

Finally, we must also point out that, while recognizing the appeal of these new products, an alternative asset management company could still prefer maintaining a managed account instead of a Newcits. In fact, in the first case, the product distribution is carried out by the platform. It has to be noted that alternative asset management companies usually have little or no experience in retail distribution of funds.

3

Analysis of the Operational Model of UCITS III Products

Although the UCITS III directive was adopted by the European Parliament in 2001, it took years for both investment companies and management companies to develop and introduce this type of product to the market. This development was rather heterogeneous due to the different ways in which Member States acknowledged the directive as well as to the different fiscal regimes concerning mutual funds.

Countries like Luxembourg, France, Ireland and the UK were favoured, while others, such as Italy, were penalized, because a fiscal regime providing taxation on accrued profits rather than on cash values is still in force, even if under revision. Indeed, the most common operational model is now the one adopted by SICAV, whose net equity is split in several tranches pursuing different investment policies and issuing different categories of shares, according to the type of investor.

3.1 LUXEMBOURG SICAVs

Once the 20 December 2002 Act had been approved, Luxembourg was the first European regulatory framework to acknowledge the contents of the UCITS III directive about UCITS. In particular, innovations brought by UCITS III to the SICAV discipline concerned both their investment possibilities and their structure, introducing a distinction between hetero-managed SICAVs (managed by a managing company) and "self-managed" SICAVs, and enumerating the requirements for their establishment. According to the type of financial instrument in which the company's assets are invested, the Luxembourg regulation provides for a division of UCIs in two categories: "SICAV

Part I" (harmonized) and "SICAV Part II" (non-harmonized), explained below. The acknowledgement of the UCITS III dispositions by Luxembourg brought relevant effects to the structure and practicality of the SICAV Part I. It then influenced the SICAV Part II insofar as, after the broadening of the investment possibilities of SICAV Part I, some of them, previously included in the discipline of Part II, were moved to Part I, acquiring the status of harmonized products.

3.1.1   Harmonized and Non-Harmonized UCITS

Part I of the 20 December 2002 Act concerns "harmonized" UCITS, i.e. those particular UCITS meeting the structure and investment policy requirements prescribed by the European directives. This kind of UCITS differentiates from others because, once the authorization by the Vigilance Authority of Luxembourg has been obtained, their shares can be freely marketed in the other EU countries.

SICAV Part I is formally defined as the Luxembourg-based *"société anonyme"*, whose shares are addressed to public placement by a public or private offer, and its exclusive business is investing in non-property assets and other financial activities cited in Article 41, paragraph (1) of the same act, with the aim of dividing the investment risk and rewarding its shareholders by the operating result, and whose share capital is always equal to the value of the company's net assets.

Since the dispositions of the UCITS III directive broadened the range of activities in which the assets of a harmonized UCITS can be invested, SICAV Part I can invest, in currency market securities, bank deposits, derivatives and shares of other funds, as well as in non-property assets, with less severe limits than previously allowed.

On the other hand, Part II of the 20 December 2002 Act regulates non-harmonized UCIs. UCIs investing in different securities from non-property assets or other financial activities cited in Article 41(1) of the same Act belong to this category, as well as the following UCITS excluded from Part I:

• Closed UCITS;

- UCITS raising funds without public promotional activities;
- UCITS that are designed to be reserved to the public of extra-UE countries;
- Other UCITS provided by CSSF whose investment policy does not meet the rules set in Article 41 and following.

Therefore, these UCIs do not benefit from the "European passport" and their shares can be marketed in another EU country only if the requirements set by the local authorities are met.

3.1.2   Self-Managed and Hetero-Managed SICAVs

The UCITS III directive allows the structure of the investment vehicle to be defined in two different ways:

- A "self-managed" SICAV, meeting the strictest law requirements;
- A "hetero-managed" SICAV, where the assets are entrusted to an external management company that will have to meet the same requirements provided for "self-managed" SICAVs.

As these management companies meet the predicted requirements (as in the 2001/107/CE directive), they are provided with a "European passport" and are then recognized as "harmonized management companies". Regarding this aspect, the 20 December 2002 Act (actually carried out by the CSSF circulars No. 03/108 and No. 05/185) introduced some conditions whose compliance is necessary to get the authorization to perform mutual investment management activities. These conditions are in force both for self-managed SICAV (Art. 27) and harmonized management companies (Art. 77). In brief, to establish a self-managed SICAV in Luxembourg it is necessary to meet the requirements reported in Table 3.1.

Moreover, the self-managed SICAV has to:

- always comply with the prudence rules set by CSSF;
- adopt a structure so that the risk of conflicts of interest is minimized;

Table 3.1 Requirements of a self-managed SICAV

Share Capital	• Must be at least €300,000 at the moment of authorization and at least €1,250,000 million within the next 6 months.
Legal and Administrative Headquarters	• Both placed in Luxembourg. This usually implies that the company must have at its disposal permanent personnel, qualified according to the roles to be accomplished and remunerated by the SICAV.
Required Documentation	• Activity programme to be introduced to the CSSF, providing a description of the company's organizational structure and its risk management practice.
SICAV Executives	• At least one of them must be placed in Luxembourg. At least two of them have to meet specific requirements, in terms of professional conduct, according to the type of activity they are going to execute. • The disclosure of the executives' names and requirements is compulsory. They cannot be chosen from amongst the employees of the SICAV depository bank.

- keep a good administrative and accounting organization;
- provide control and security devices in the IT area;
- provide adequate mechanisms of internal control in order to check and regulate the employees' personal activities, to guarantee that the assets are invested according to the constitutional documents and law dispositions, and to provide complete traceability of any transaction in terms of origin, involved parties, nature, time and place.

Concerning self-managed SICAVs, a minimum initial capital of €31,000 is required, which will have to increase to €1,250,000 within the 6 months following the authorization. The capital of the management company will not have to be lower than €125,000, plus an amount compounded as percentage of the managed assets. In this case, the SICAV asset is included in the determination of the asset's suitability requisites of the management company, since the capital requirements applying are proportional to the managed assets.

The 20 December 2002 Act does not provide further information about the establishment of a hetero-managed SICAV. In this case, only the management company is supposed to meet the requirements prescribed by the law. On the contrary, the hetero-managed SICAV is released from the predict requirements. These dispositions, included in Part I of the Act, apply without distinction both to self-managed and hetero-managed SICAVs, though in the different organizational structure.

3.2   CSSF 07/308 CIRCULAR: GUIDELINES FOR LUXEMBOURG UCITS

The 07/308 circular is addressed to the UCITS that are subject to Part I of the 20 December 2002 Act, i.e. the so-called "harmonized" UCITS, with the aim of identifying further criteria about financial risk management and the use of derivative securities. Circular 07/308 applies to all the Luxembourg UCITS and to all the companies involved in their management or supervision. The main suggestions of the circular are:

- definition of guidelines to implement a risk management process, including organizational principles and the activities of the risk management unit;
- introduction of "sophisticated" and "non-sophisticated" UCITS;
- definition of risk limits for sophisticated and non-sophisticated UCITS, particularly focusing on market risk (or *global risk*), counterparty risk and concentration risk;
- definition of the coverage rules applicable to derivatives;
- definition of "reliable and verifiable" valuation of OTC contracts;
- information concerning the structure of the risk management unit to be communicated to CSSF.

CSSF entrusts to every single UCITS the faculty to classify itself as sophisticated or non-sophisticated. Generally, sophisticated UCITS use, for a relevant part of their investments, derivative securities or other strategies and more complex securities. On the contrary, non-sophisticated UCTIS adopt less complex strategies and use derivative securities only for protection purposes.

Concerning the estimation of *global exposure*, counterparty and concentration risks, the main differences between sophisticated and non-sophisticated UCITS are the following:

- Non-sophisticated UCITS have to measure and check financial risks linked to their investments at least once in 2 months, while sophisticated UCITS have to perform this check on a daily basis.
- Regarding the estimation of the global exposure, non-sophisticated UCITS should, in principle, adopt the commitment approach, while sophisticated UCITS have to use an internal model approach and take into consideration both general and specific market risk. The VAR methodology is the most common internal model approach.

3.2.1 Structure of the Risk Management Unit

Article 42 of the 20 December 2002 Act requires UCITS to implement a risk management methodology allowing them to monitor and measure at any time the risk of every position and its contribution to the general risk profile. Then circular 07/308 sets the criteria that sophisticated and non-sophisticated UCITS have to follow to implement an efficient risk management process.

Sophisticated UCITS

Sophisticated UCITS have to assign the role of identifying, measuring, monitoring and checking risks associated with portfolio positions to a risk management unit, independent from the units in which portfolio decisions are taken. In order to satisfy the Commission's requests, the risk management unit has to meet the following five qualitative requirements:

- The unit's personnel must be numerically sufficient and sufficiently skilled.
- The risk management unit has to own the necessary IT instruments to perform its functions.
- People managing the management company's business must be actively involved in the risk management and control process. Their role is to approve the risk management and control method.
- The risk management unit has to account directly to the business managers, which must be periodically updated by reports including information about the unit's job and the risk borne by UCITS. It is at the discretion of the business managers to take adequate decisions based on the reported information.
- The boards of directors of the management and investment companies have the responsibility to ensure that the risk management unit abides by laws and regulations, and that the implemented mechanisms work properly.

These requirements must also be met by the non-sophisticated UCITS making use of the internal model. The Commission allows the management companies or the self-managed investment companies to delegate the risk management process, fully or partially, to skilled third parties. In any case, third parties must meet the same requirements as the risk management unit. The delegation of these functions does not relieve the management company or the investment company of their responsibility.

Non-Sophisticated UCITS

In the case of non-sophisticated UCITS, the organizational structure of the risk management unit should not be as developed or as complex as that of the sophisticated UCITS, unless internal model-type procedures of risk control are in force. Therefore, the Commission allows the UCITS to delegate the risk management function to the unit managing portfolio decisions (or front office). In order to guarantee an adequate degree of independence, a third and independent entity can take charge of the activities of the risk management unit. Finally, the Commission can also ask non-sophisticated UCITS to meet the requirements of sophisticated UCITS, when considering it appropriate.

3.2.2   Activities of the Risk Management Unit

The role of the risk management unit is to monitor the overall exposure, the counterparty and concentration risks associated with every portfolio position. In this context, it is necessary to pay attention to transactions involving derivative securities, provided the specific risks (leverage effect, high volatility of market prices, complexity, etc.) are linked to these categories of securities.

The CSSF expects the risk management unit to perform the activities reported in Table 3.2.

3.2.3   Determination of the Global Exposure for Non-Sophisticated UCITS

For non-sophisticated UCITS, the global exposure related to derivative securities only, must be determined according to the commitment approach. This implies that, for a given position in a derivative security, the commitment approach-based calculation converts this position to an equivalent one on the underlying of the same derivative security. This conversion process must be implemented for all derivative securities, as reported in Table 3.3.

Total commitment regarding positions in derivative securities is limited to 100% of NAV and is calculated as the absolute value of the sum of the commitments on each derivative security. Any possible netting or hedging effect must be taken into account, on which basis some derivative securities could be excluded from the commitment calculation (point III.2). CSSF included in Appendix 1 of the 07/3080 circular the calculation method for the most common derivatives. In

Table 3.2 Activities performed by the risk management unit.

Point III.1	• Determination and control of the global exposure.
Point III.2	• Determination and control of the counterparty risk linked to OTC derivative securities.
Points III.1 and III.2, Appendix 1 and 2	• Control and maintenance of the minimum requisites for the determination of global exposure and counterparty risk.
Point III.3	• Determination and control of the concentration limits usage.
Point IV.1	• Monitoring and control of the "coverage rules"
Point IV.2	• Determination and control, if applicable, of the valuation of OTC derivative securities.
. . .	• Preparation of risk control reports for business managers of the management company or SIAG.

case UCITS makes use of other securities, the calculation method must be disclosed to CSSF and set in concert with it.

Netting and Position Coverage Process

Applying the commitment approach, UCITS can implement the following netting typologies:

• Netting between buy and sell positions of derivative securities on the same underlying, independent of the expiry date.
• Netting between derivative securities and UCITS-owned assets, on condition that the two positions refer to the same underlying.

Moreover, it is possible to exclude from the commitment calculation those derivative securities whose purpose is to cover portfolio

Table 3.3 Commitment calculation for the main categories of derivative securities

Instrument	Commitment calculation
Share options	Number of contracts × Number of shares × Underlying price × Option's delta.
Bond options	Number of contracts × Nominal value × Underlying price × Option's delta.
Warrant	Number of contracts × Number of shares × Underlying price × Option's delta.
Future on index	Number of contracts ×) One point value × Index value
Future on bonds	Number of contracts × Face value of future contract × Future market value.
Forward contract	Contract principal.
Interest rate swap	Contract principal.
Credit default swap (protection buyer)	Sum of coupons to pay during the whole contract duration.
Credit default swap (protection seller)	Face value of the contract.
Currency swap	Contract principal.

positions from market risk fluctuations. This possibility is strictly limited to the cases in which this risk reduction is undeniable – for example, when the prices of one or more positions, and the position in derivatives, move in opposite directions, or when the covered assets and the derivatives' underlying are adequately similar.

The netting can be performed only for equivalent commitments, both in terms of market value and risk (e.g. duration), and cannot lead to any negligence by UCITS towards clear tangible risks. Finally, the netting process has to be monitored by the risk management unit.

3.2.4 Determination of the Global Exposure for Sophisticated UCITS

The Commission requires that all UCITS pursuing a sophisticated investment strategy adopt an internal model-based approach, considering every exposure source (general and specific market risk) that could significantly affect the portfolio value. As the internal model, the Commission refers to a *Value-at-Risk* type model, like *Relative VAR, Absolute VAR* or *Monte Carlo VAR.*

Relative VAR Approach

By the Relative VAR approach, the global exposure calculation for UCITS must be performed through the following steps:

- First, it is necessary to calculate the VAR of the current UCITS portfolio (including also derivative securities).
- Second, a reference portfolio, not leveraged and not including derivative securities, must be identified. The VAR associated with this portfolio must be calculated with the same criteria adopted in Step 1.
- Finally, it is necessary to check that the VAR associated with the UCITS portfolio does not double the VAR of the reference portfolio. In this way, a limit of 2 in the portfolio leverage is ensured.

The global exposure resulting from the application of this methodology is then below 100% and calculated according to the following formula:

$$\frac{Var(UCITS) - Var(Reference\ portfolio)}{Var(Reference\ portfolio)} \times 100$$

However, this approach shows some limits, since additional adjustments may be necessary to ensure compliance with the global exposure limits defined by the UCITS directive. Indeed, the VAR may not be a fit instrument to value all risks deriving from UCITS, and the choice of a reference portfolio is a rather tricky task.

For example, let's suppose that a UCITS invests 100% of its net asset in the European stock market and assumes additional synthetic positions equal to 120% long and 120% short on the same market. In most cases, the global exposure calculation by the commitment approach could provide a result equal to 240% of NAV. On the other hand, depending on the VAR method adopted (historical or Monte Carlo) and market data, the overall portfolio VAR may result below the double VAR of a European stock reference portfolio.

Finally, the VAR of some reference portfolios could be rather high and, once doubled, could produce high risk levels. The accepted VAR in these cases can be higher than the absolute VAR thresholds imposed by the Member States.

Absolute VAR Approach

An alternative methodology that a sophisticated UCITS could adopt for the calculation of the global exposure is the Absolute VAR approach, on which base a maximum VAR value is set in terms of NAV percentage. Since this type of measure is not compared to a reference derivatives-free portfolio, as in the Relative VAR approach, it is important to set a sufficiently conservative VAR limit, portraying the limits imposed to UCITS concerning an issuer's default risk.

Since the VAR measures the worst expected loss for a given confidence level in a certain period of time, a proposal has been brought arguing that the absolute VAR, calculated with a 99% confidence level and a 20 working days holding period, was below 20% of UCITS' NAV. This limit can be compared to the loss risk of 20% deriving from the concentration towards a single issuer.

Despite the threshold being defined for a specific time period and a certain confidence level, both these parameters are "scalable", up and down. Therefore, the UCITS can use different confidence levels and holding periods, subsequently scaling the VAR obtained on the parameters set in the directive. In this case, the UCITS must convert the VAR limit into a new threshold based on the chosen parameters, assuming that the UCITS returns are independent and normally distributed, and adopting the concordance results reported in Table 3.4.

Hence, the VAR at the $y\%$ level can be obtained by multiplying the VAR at the $x\%$ level with the ratio between the coefficients

Table 3.4 Concordance table

Confidence level	Normal distribution coefficient
99%	2.326
97.5%	1.96
95%	1.645
90%	1.282

of the normal distribution at the $y\%$ and $x\%$ levels, respectively. For example, if the UCITS in its control process adopts a 95% confidence level, it can calculate its VAR at a 99% level through the following method:

$$VAR(99\%) \approx VAR(95\%) \times \frac{2.326}{1.645}$$

The same method allows us to convert the VAR associated with an m-day holding period in a VAR with the same confidence level and an n-day period, using the square root of time:

$$VAR(n \, days) \approx VAR(m \, days) \times \frac{\sqrt{n}}{\sqrt{m}}$$

For example:

$$VAR(5 \, days, 95\%) \approx VAR(20 \, days, 95\%) \times \frac{\sqrt{5}}{\sqrt{20}}$$

The following example shows that setting a limit at 20% of NAV for the VAR at a 99% confidence level and a 20-day holding period is equivalent to requiring a VAR at a 95% level and a 5-day holding period lower than 7% of NAV.

$$VAR(5 \, days, 95\%) \approx VAR(20 \, days, 99\%) \times \frac{\sqrt{5}}{\sqrt{20}}$$

$$\times \frac{1.645}{2.326} \leq 7\% \times NAV$$

The Absolute VAR method measures the portfolio potential loss but does not provide suggestions about the leverage. Hence, the use of this method implies the risk that the UCITS is also allowed to adopt highly levered strategies even in the presence of an inadequate risk management system, without considering the *fat tail risk*.

For example, UCITS using arbitrage strategies in which the combination of long and short strategies simultaneously involves the presence of thick tails in the return distribution, and a low VAR, could actually include very high degrees of leverage.

Additional devices to check the risk profile (such as stress-testing, CVAR or other methods able to define the potential impact of low probability market events) are required for those UCITS adopting the predicted strategies and calculating their global exposure through the Absolute VAR approach.

The purpose of the VAR model is to quantify the highest potential loss that could be generated by a UCITS portfolio in normal market conditions. The loss estimation is based on a certain time period and a given confidence interval. A UCITS must integrate this approach with a stress test, as described in Appendix 2 of the 07/308 CSSF circular, in order to quantify the risks associated with possible anomalous market movements. These tests evaluate the reactions of the portfolio value in case of extreme financial or economic events in a given moment.

However, other risk quantification methods meeting the requirements listed in this document can be accepted by the Commission. If the VAR does not seem to be fit for a UCITS because of the nature of the risks to which it is exposed, the Commission expects the UCITS to adopt other risk measurement methods. In all these cases, the Commission's preliminary opinion is required.

3.2.5   The Counterparty Risk

Article 43(1) of the 20 December 2002 Act argues that the exposure towards a counterparty in an OTC transaction cannot exceed 10% of the owned assets if the counterparty is a bank appointed by Art.

41(1)(f), or 5% otherwise. Moreover, Art. 43(2) argues that a UCITS cannot invest more than 20% of its assets in one of the following combinations:

- investment in non-property assets or currency market instruments issued by a single counterparty;
- deposits in a single counterparty;
- exposures deriving from OTC derivative transactions subscribed with a single counterparty.

The counterparty of an OTC transaction, as well as being skilled in this specific transaction category, must be subject to prudency supervision and belong to one of the categories approved by the Commission. The counterparty risk calculation can be divided into three stages:

- The UCITS defines the present value of substitution of the derivatives included in the portfolio, performing a valuation at market prices. Only positive substitution costs are considered.
- The UCITS sets their potential future credit risk multiplying the *principal notional* or the underlying assets of all contracts (also considering those with negative substitution costs) for a so called *add-on* factor. Add-on factors are fixed in the circular (Table 3.5) and depend on the underlying nature and the time to contract expiry.
- The sum of the substitution present value and the potential future credit risk is multiplied for a weighting factor equal to 20% for European banks and investment companies, or 50% otherwise.

Table 3.5 Add-on factors

Residual term	Interest rate derivatives	Exchange rate derivatives	Ownership derivatives	Other derivatives
Less than 1 month	0%	1%	6%	10%
From 1 to 5 years	0.5%	5%	8%	12%
More than 5 years	1.5%	7.5%	10%	15%

The result of this calculation is then divided by the UCITS' NAV and this ratio must be lower than 10% when the counterparty is a bank, or 5% otherwise.

3.2.6   Limits of Concentration Risk

UCITS can invest in derivative securities if the aggregate underlying exposure does not exceed the investment limits set by the 20 December 2002 Act. This is often called the "look-through principle". Derivatives must be converted in equivalent positions on the respective underlying using, in principle, the calculation methods given in Appendix 1 of the 07/308 circular. Derivatives included in non-property assets or currency market instruments must be isolated for the estimation of the concentration risk.

3.3   SWING PRICING

The huge redemptions received by hedge funds at the end of 2009 have introduced an important fairness issue in the treatment of investors. Indeed, in the presence of huge redemptions and low market liquidity (high bid–ask spreads) continuing investors bear unwinding portfolio costs. However, it should be desirable that only redeeming investors are incurred in these costs. For this purpose, the swing pricing is an alternative NAV calculation method that creates fairness of treatment between continuing investors and redeeming investors. It does not deal with a subscription fee or a redemption fee, but with a new industry standard introduced in order to protect existing investors and let the subscribing or redeeming investors be the only ones bearing the portfolio unwinding costs. Another CSSF circular particularly relevant for the definition of the hedge fund operating model is 04/146, related to "Market Timing and Late Trading".

In particular, this document faces a typical issue regarding open funds investors, i.e. the dilution of the fund's value (and then of the share), after the transaction costs arising when the portfolio manager reallocates the fund's asset due to a net flow of subscriptions or redemptions. Indeed, if subscription demand is higher than the redemption demand (or vice versa) and there is a net positive incoming (or outgoing) flow, the portfolio manager must address the market to rebalance the ratio between fund value and number of shares, creating transaction costs.

However, the assignment of these transaction costs is unfair, since they have not been created by continuing investors (investors remaining invested in the fund), but by active shareholders, i.e. investors who recently joined or left. This inequality is caused by the fact that the price at which investors buy and sell fund shares (NAV) reflects exclusively the value of its assets. The suggested method – to protect continuing investors from dilution – consists in changing the fund's NAV to take into account the capital movement costs, so that they can be correctly allocated to active shareholders.

Once the capital net flow is known, it is possible to apply one of the following methods:

• Full swing pricing: the NAV is adjusted on a daily basis, according to subscriptions or redemptions, related to the net capital flow size.

Partial swing pricing: the process of NAV adjustment is activated only when the net capital flow exceeds a predetermined threshold called the "swing threshold".

The NAV's oscillating direction will then depend on the direction of the capital net flow:

• Positive net incoming flow: the NAV used to manage the transactions is adjusted upward.
• Positive net outgoing flow: the NAV used to manage the transactions is adjusted downward.

From an inspection of Figure 3.1 it can be seen that – under the hypothesis that the fund's performance remains unchanged during the considered period – the application of swing pricing implies a

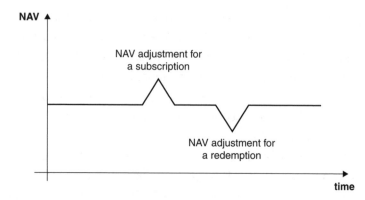

Figure 3.1 Swing pricing effect on NAV

temporary variation of the NAV value due to subscriptions or re-demptions. This also determines an increase in NAV volatility.

For example, let's assume that the bid–ask spread is 75 basis points, that yesterday's NAV was 100, and that today's fund performance is 0%. For investors subscribing today, the NAV will be adjusted according to swing pricing, so the entry for NAV will be 100.75. This implies that the number of shares to be received is lower than the case of a NAV of 100. Tomorrow the NAV will return to 100, assuming that the fund performance is still 0%.

3.3.1   The Swing Factor

The swing factor is the size of the variation applied to the NAV, so it represents the transaction costs borne by the portfolio manager. The aspects considered in the swing factor calculation are, in order of importance:

- the bid–ask spread of NAV's underlying securities (or its estima-tion);
- net negotiation commissions;
- custody expenses;
- fiscal duties;
- any other cost related to currency markets, if relevant.

3.3.2 Pros and Cons of Swing Pricing

Benefits coming from the swing-pricing technique can be summarized as follows:

- It is complementary to single-priced funds, i.e. those funds using a unique price to represent the value of their own assets and therefore not providing bid-ask spreads.
- It protects long-term investors from dilution.
- It discourages frequent trading and market timing.
- It also applies to funds with multiple share classes.

However this technique is affected by the following disadvantages:

- The division of transaction costs between active shareholders is often unequal, both regarding the transaction direction and the volume generated by the single investor.
- It can affect informational transparency towards investors.
- It can increase short-term volatility.

It can increase tracking errors.

- It can distort the calculation of the performance fee.
- In the case of multiple share classes, the global activity can be anything that is considered.

The first disadvantage concerns the unequal distribution of transaction costs among active shareholders and the subsequent dilution, though less relevant than before. Indeed, it is true that active shareholders making transactions in the direction of the capital net flow are affected by dilution, while in the opposite direction they receive a benefit from the use of swing pricing. Moreover, all active shareholders suffering dilution are affected in the same way, irrespective of the traded volumes of capital.

Table 3.6 Full swing pros and cons

Full swing advantages	Full swing disadvantages
Transparent and easy to understand.	Increase of NAV's volatility.
Substantial transaction processing during each negotiation day.	Thin net flows of capital can be covered by cash put aside by the fund. Therefore the NAV variation is not always justified, since the fund does not always incur transaction costs.
It always has positive effects on the fund.	Increase of the risk for NAV to be modified in the wrong direction or that some transactions are processed by mistake, due to delays in acquisition of the data on capital movements.

3.3.3   Pros and Cons of Full and Partial Swing

Subsequent to the decision to implement the swing pricing technique, it is necessary to consider, case by case, the most appropriate method to adopt on the basis of its related advantages and disadvantages (see Tables 3.6 and 3.7).

Table 3.7 Partial swing pros and cons

Partial swing advantages.	Partial swing disadvantages.
Since the net flow of capital must exceed a given threshold before the NAV could be modified, the risk of mistakes in NAV calculation is lower than adopting full swing.	Increase of NAV's volatility.
Since NAV is not modified every single negotiation day, the impact on NAV's volatility is lower.	

3.3.4   Operational Implications

First, it is important to consider the implications concerning NAV production and publication, in order to prevent misunderstandings with the information's recipients. This is also true for production and publication schedules, that will be necessarily delayed by the adoption of swing pricing.

Another important implication is the determination of the swing factor and of the swing threshold, which should be the responsibility of the board of directors. Even if the fund's prospectus describes the implementation mechanisms of swing pricing, there is no obligation to reveal any details related to the swing factor or swing threshold that would produce a transparency issue in its implementation. Moreover, it is possible to establish a committee for periodical checks and confirmation of these factors.

Finally, an implication that must be considered is that any fee estimated relative to NAV will have to be calculated *ex ante* the implementation of the swing factor, otherwise a significant distortion occurs.

3.4   DEPOSITARY BANK, ADMINISTRATOR AND LACK OF PRIME BROKER

According to Article 7 of the 85/611/CEE directive, the custody of the assets of the mutual investment fund must be entrusted to a depositary bank – that is, an independent bank designated to keep the fund's financial securities and cash, and check compliance with the investment guidelines. If anomalies are found in the administration of the management company or fund management, the depositary bank must notify such findings to the management company and to the authorities. In general, according to the predicted article, the depositary bank's tasks can be summarized as follows:

- Check that the selling, issuing, repurchase, redemption or with-drawal of the shares performed on behalf of the fund or the management company are accomplished according to law or the fund's regulations.

- Check the accuracy in the calculation of the value of the fund's shares (NAV) or, on behalf of the SGR, directly calculate it.
- Execute the instructions of the management company, if they are not against the law, regulations, or the prescriptions of the vigilance authorities.
- Check that, in the transactions involving the fund's assets, the equivalent value is remitted in the terms of use.
- Check that the fund's revenues are assigned according to legal requirements or fund value.

The depositary bank is also subject to the requirements listed in Table 3.8.

3.4.1 The Role of the Administrator

The administrator is a third party, independent from the manager, commissioned by the fund to calculate the same fund's NAV. Sometimes the administrator's role may coincide with that of the depositary bank. The administrator's independence is a necessary condition to avoid conflicts of interest for the manager when valuing the fund's securities.

The administrator evaluates fund's securities according to a defined valuation policy based on FAS (Financial Accounting Standards) principles. First, the different asset categories are classified in three levels on the degree of certainty by which their value can be calculated.

Level 1 assets can be valued with certainty, since their liquidity is sufficiently high and market prices are clear and always available. Level 1 assets include, for example, shares and bonds or derivative securities listed and frequently traded in a stock market.

Level 2 assets are financial instruments valued on the basis of trading on less active markets, or securities whose value is built on a model based on inputs that are always observable, both directly and indirectly, for the entire duration of the security. Examples of

Table 3.8 Depositary bank's requirements

Registered office [Art. 8(1)]	• The depositary bank must place its own registered office in the Member State in which the management company has its registered office, or it must be established there if its registered office is in another Member State.
Public control [Art. 8 (2)]	• The depositary bank must be subject to public control. It must provide sufficient financial and professional guarantees to enable it to effectively accomplish tasks and commitments deriving from its depositary role. • The Member States set the categories from which depositary banks can be chosen.
Responsibility towards investors [Art. 9]	• The depositary bank is responsible, according to the national right of the Member State in which the management company's registered office is situated, to the management company and the participants, for any prejudice deriving from negligence or wrong compliance of its obligations. In the case of participants, the responsibility can be direct or indirect through the management company, based on the legal relationships between the depositary bank, the management company and the participants.
Depositary and management company [Art. 10(1),(2)]	• The management company and depositary roles cannot be accomplished by the same firm. • The management company and the depositary bank must act independently and exclusively in pursuance of the participants' interest.

this type of asset are, for instance, corporate bonds, municipal bonds, OTC derivatives such as interest rate swaps and currency swaps, or securities with mortgages or loans as their underlying.

Finally, level 3 assets are illiquid securities whose valuation is based on management assumptions, since the variables needed to estimate their fair value are not observable. Level 3 assets can include some categories of mortgage-related securities, or complex derivatives such as long-term options, weakly traded and with no reliable market price.

Regarding the valuation methodologies of these activities, FAS 157 introduces the following indications:

- Clear definition of the notion of fair value;
- Classification of the sources of information used in fair value-type valuations (e.g. market based or non-market based). Broadening of the transparency requirements of the performed valuation. Consider the impact of possible credit risk variation (both of the counterparty and the same company) in the valuation.

FAS 157 provides a definition of fair value as the amount receivable by selling an asset (or the amount payable to transfer an own debt) through a market transaction at a specified date. The same notion of fair value implies that the valuation is based on a hypothetical "exit price", rather than on the purchase price, no matter if the activity will be subsequently held or sold.

FAS 157 highlights that fair value is based on the market and not on the purchase price. Therefore, the buyer's typical optimism must be replaced by the typical risk-averse buyer's scepticism.

Concerning commercial banks and other companies offering financial services, some asset categories such as derivatives and traded stocks must be priced at the fair value. For other asset categories, such as financial credits and debt securities, it depends on whether they are owned for trading or investment purpose.

All trading activities are valued at fair value. Financial credits and debt securities owned for investment purpose, or held until their maturity, are valued at amortized cost, unless they should be depreciated (in this case, a loss is reported). In any case, if these activities are going to be sold, their valuation must be performed at fair value or at the lower between the fair value and their cost (see FAS 65, 114, 115 and 159). In general, common practice requires a mark-to-market application.

In some cases the relative asset market can be poor in liquidity, as occurs for instance during periods of economical crisis. In these circumstances, there may be a lack of potential buyers, making the mark-to-market process more complicated. In the absence of market information, it is permissible to use one's personal assumptions, even if the basic concept must be the same: what would the asset's trading value be if there was a potential buyer?

In any case, it is not possible when formulating hypothesis to ignore the availability of market information such as interest rates, default rates, etc. FAS 157 makes no distinction between non-cash-generating assets (such as damaged machinery, etc., whose theoretical value would be null if no one was willing to buy them on the market) and cash-generating assets (such as financial securities, keeping a value until they generate revenues from the underlying activities).

3.4.2   The Lack of Prime Broker

In offshore hedging, the main functions of the prime broker's funds are borrowing securities (in order to allow short selling), financing (to allow leverage) and the custody of securities. The prime broker, therefore, performs trade settlement and accounts reconciliation, and does not act as a backroom officer whose tasks are partly done by the management company and the administrator. If UCITS III funds do not directly adopt leverage and short selling, they do not have a prime broker: the custody of securities is held by the depository bank.

4

Hedge Funds Investment Strategies and Limits Set by UCITS III

Hedge funds are characterized by alternative management styles or investment strategies and they differentiate according to the specialization of the market or industry. In practice, they are often managed by multiple styles, which enables them to be included in various categories at the same time. Moreover, some managers have such peculiar styles as to have unique characteristics even within the same investment strategy. In this context, the aim of this chapter is to provide a brief review of the most common hedge strategies and, according to the law and the operational model, evaluate which of them can effectively be pursued by a Newcits fund.

Based on a typical classification in the literature about alternative investments, it is possible to define five different strategies, which will be detailed later in this chapter. First, the following categories are classified, on the grounds that no classification is exhaustive, but it is helpful to better understand the wide and heterogeneous world of hedge funds:

- Long/short equity;
- Relative value;
- Directional/trading;
- Event driven (or special situation);
- Other strategies.

In long/short equity strategies, the manager purchases those shares that are supposed to be undervalued by the market, and short sells those that are overvalued. At present this is the most common strategy in hedge funds, and although it is perhaps the easiest to understand, it is also one of the most difficult to perform. This category also includes the case of equity market neutral.

The relative value strategies are arbitrage transactions whose revenue derives from the spread between two securities rather than from the general market condition. For instance, relative value strategies include convertible bond arbitrage, fixed income arbitrage and mortgage-backed arbitrage.

Directional/trading strategies try to exploit the general market tendencies rather than focus their analysis on single securities. They include the global macro and managed futures strategy.

Event-driven strategies try to gain profits from the opportunities occurring during the company's lifecycle and created by extraordinary events, such as carve-outs, mergers, acquisitions, consolidations, liquidations and reorganizations.

Finally, other strategies form a residual category, which includes those strategies that are most recent and innovative.

After discussing these five categories of strategies (4.1–4.5), we present the limits imposed by UCITS III (4.6), and two techniques currently applied by Newcits funds in order to overcome some of the more restrictive constraints, namely the case of synthetic short-selling by means of contracts for differences (4.7) and the recent phenomenon of the Synthetic Newcits (4.8).

4.1 LONG/SHORT EQUITY

Managers using this strategy have the aim of distinguishing those securities (generally shares) that they consider undervalued or overvalued by the market. They then purchase the former (assuming a long position) and short sell the latter (assuming in this case a short position). This strategy is profitable if long positions go up and short positions go down; if the reverse occurs, it suffers losses. Portfolio coverage can also be provided without short selling, for example, using derivatives on stock indices: it is a frequent practice, indeed, to sell futures on stock indices to rapidly vary portfolio exposure related to the changed market conditions. Managers adopting this strategy make use of the same fundamental, technical and statistical analyses employed by traditional equity managers and trade on the same reference market. A hedge fund, however, is structurally distinguished from a traditional mutual fund by short selling, leverage and the manager's incentive system. In a long/short portfolio, short positions have a double advantage: they provide a negative exposure to securities that are believed to be overvalued and they reduce the portfolio's market exposure by hedging the systematic risk. A portfolio managed along the long/short equity style can take four main positions:

- straight long, namely, long positions on the stock of companies appreciated by the manager (e.g. a long position on General Electric);
- straight short, namely, short positions on the stock of companies not appreciated by the manager (e.g. a short position on Intel);
- share class arbitrage, consisting in arbitrage between the different share categories of a certain company, such as ordinary, privileged and preferred shares;
- pair trades, namely, a position on the relative strengths of two securities (e.g. long Deutsche Telekom versus short Vodafone).

The net market exposure equals the sum of the weights of the long positions less the absolute value of the sum of the weights of the short positions, while the gross market exposure equals the sum of the weights of the long positions plus the absolute value of the sum of the weights of the short positions. It is important to remark that a hedge fund with a net market exposure equal to zero is not hedged: on the contrary, its manager might lose money on both the long and the short positions, and so actually lose much more rapidly than a traditional fund. On the other hand, the gross market exposure tells us how much money the manager has actually put at risk.

The manager can decide to hold a deliberate positive overall market exposure (net long bias) to take advantage of a generalized bullish period; he may hold a negative net exposure (net short bias); or he may vary the net exposure (variable bias). Generally, the net market exposure is positive (long bias), even though occasionally some funds, driven by the manager's strong macroeconomic view, may have a net short exposure. As a result, the performance of long/short equity hedge funds tends to show a positive correlation to the performance of the reference equity markets. When markets are bearish, these types of funds generally tend to be negatively correlated, and yet outperform the market. The hedge fund's manager can assume a bottom-up, top-down or stereoscopic approach:

- Bottom-up, when the manager deeply examines the fundamentals of individual companies and selects those he wishes to buy or short sell. Typically, these managers are stock-pickers.
- Top-down, when the manager assumes his positions on the basis of a macroeconomic view, deciding the geographical and industry allocation first, and only then selecting securities. Typically, these managers follow an industry rotation, trying to anticipate the market's industrial preference depending on the economic cycle.
- Stereoscopic, when the manager combines the two predicted approaches.

Moreover, there are different approaches according to the investment perspective adopted. The value style is based on the analysis of the fundamentals of the listed companies. Value managers seek to identify companies whose intrinsic value has not yet been appreciated by the market: companies whose potential has not been recognized by the market; companies that trade under the sum-of-the-parts evaluation; or companies that trade at discounted market multiples compared to peer companies. Many managers prefer to use liquidity measures rather than accounting measures. In addition, a widely used indicator is the so-called director dealing, i.e. dealing in their company's shares by top management. Although it is true that top managers can sell their company's shares for many reasons, there is only one reason why they buy: when they believe that their company's shares are undervalued. In any case, even if a stock is strongly undervalued, it may remain so for a long time unless catalytic events take place, clearly revealing to the market the downward bias: if a manager invests in a similar stock, he may be caught in the so-called value trap.

Momentum managers seek to gain profits from the so-called performance persistence effect, by which securities, industries and markets that have overperformed will continue to do so. This means that they set a position in order to leverage the trend persistence. When a trend reversal occurs, the possible market excesses are wiped out. This is the so-called mean reversion effect, leading some managers to behave differently from their colleagues, by trying to anticipate trend reversals (counter trend or contrarian).

Finally, long/short equity managers can specialize in a reference market, or in a reference economic area, depending on the manager's field of expertise that, in his opinion, provides him with a competitive advantage over his competitors.

4.1.1   Equity Market Neutral

A long/short equity strategy variation is the one used by equity market-neutral funds, characterized by holding a market neutral portfolio, i.e. its performance is independent of market movements. Even though they are close relatives, equity market-neutral funds differ from long/short equity funds by the level of their systematic risk. During a market uptrend, equity market-neutral funds make a profit if long positions go up more rapidly than the drop in value incurred by the short positions in a portfolio. On the other hand, in a market downtrend, they make profits if short positions go up at a faster rate than the rate at which long positions are going down. A beta-adjusted net exposure close to zero is a target for every truly equity market-neutral portfolio. Notwithstanding, an equity market-neutral portfolio may have a beta-adjusted net exposure that is very close to zero, but its beta-adjusted net exposure with regard to industries or geographical areas will not be zero, and therefore it may be subject to specific risk, for example sector risks or country risks. However, the consequence of dropping any systemic exposure risk is that the objective of maximising performances has to be abandoned.

4.2   RELATIVE VALUE

Relative value strategies are arbitrage trades whose revenue comes from the spread between the two securities rather than the general market trend. Among relative value strategies, we present in this section convertible bond arbitrage, fixed income arbitrage and mortgage-backed arbitrage.

4.2.1 Convertible Bond Arbitrage

Convertible bonds are bonds that give their holders the right to periodic coupon payments and, as of a fixed date, the right to convert the bonds into a fixed number of shares. In most cases, these shares are common stock of the issuer, yet sometimes it can be shares from another company, should the issuer decide to sell an equity investment it holds in another company by issuing a convertible.

Convertibles are ideal securities for arbitrage because the convertible itself, namely the underlying stock and the associated derivatives, are traded along predictable ratios and any discrepancy or misprice would give rise to arbitrage opportunities for hedge fund managers.

The largest part of arbitrage trades on convertible bonds is performed through a long position on the convertible bond, hedged with a simultaneous short sale of the underlying common stock. The goal of the hedge fund manager is thus to identify convertible bonds that have a substantial market price difference compared to the theoretical value and to carry out trades that allow him to extract that value, while being protected against market risks. Generally, the risk of interest rate fluctuations is hedged on the convertible long position by using interest rate swaps, and sometimes the convertible issuer's credit risk is also hedged against (risk that the spread widens and issuer default risk) by resorting to credit default swaps.

A hedge fund manager can establish various types of arbitrages:

- Cash flow arbitrage: a hedge fund manager buying a convertible bond and short selling the underlying stock is constructing a position that generates a high cash flow. The proceeds from the stock short sale are used to finance the purchase of the convertible bond. Cash flow arbitrage is actively used in situations where there is no bond floor – for example, in mandatory convertibles, because they have a higher coupon compared to a convertible bond and generally have a similar risk to that of the stock. The static return is represented by the payment of the fixed coupon – i.e. the return from the cash proceeds generated by the short sale, which may be decreased by the payment of dividends and the cost of leverage.

- Volatility trading: most convertible bond arbitrages are constructed with a long position on the convertible and a concurrent short position on the underlying share for a fixed number of shares defined by the delta of the convertible. The hedge ratio is the number of shares that must be short sold to get a delta-neutral portfolio of convertibles and shares. A delta-neutral position yields positive returns irrespective of whether the stock goes up or down: this is determined by the fact that the delta rises when the stock goes up and declines when the stock goes down. The different variables affecting the price of the convertible start changing once the initial position has been constructed, therefore the fund manager must constantly adjust the hedge to remain delta neutral. This constant adjusting of the hedge to keep the portfolio delta neutral is called delta hedging.

- Gamma trading: in addition to delta trading, hedge fund managers can capture an additional profit by trading the underlying stock in response to delta changes. The gamma of a convertible bond is the convertible's delta sensitivity to changes in the underlying stock price. Gamma hedging or gamma trading is the delta hedge adjustment process in response to market movements; fund managers gamma hedge to capture the volatility/profit of the underlying stock.

- Credit arbitrage: hedge fund managers transfer the interest rate risk and eventually the stock option risk to other counterparties by using swaps. They will make a profit if the issuer's credit quality improves over time, or if it worsens over time as anticipated by the fund manager. With a credit default swap and an interest rate swap, it is possible indeed to break the convertible bond down into its components: call option on the stock, floating and fixed rate bond.

- Skewed arbitrage: this strategy is available to macro hedge funds, and allows the fund manager to construct a bearish position with a limited downside risk and with a long time horizon.

- Carry trade: this consists of buying bonds with a higher yield than the money you borrowed to buy them; higher yields are associated with higher risks.
- Refinancing play: these are convertible bonds that are held for their high credit spread, whereby the expected catalyst event is the announcement of a new financing plan, which can dispel doubts on the issuer's ability to meet its redemption obligations at maturity of the convertible bond. The fundamental analysis of the issuer's credit position allows the hedge fund manager to form an opinion on the likelihood that the company is going to look for a new financing.
- Late stage restructuring play: when a company undergoes a restructuring, most convertible holders are distressed investors, who bought at lower prices and are now seeking to make profits and move somewhere else. Generally, buyers are very rare because the picture of the issuer's recent distress is still vivid, resulting in few buyers in a market where there are many sellers. This leaves hedge fund managers with the possibility of reaping market opportunities.
- Multistrategy: this approach includes all the arbitrage techniques analysed up to this point.

4.2.2   Fixed Income Arbitrage

- Diverse trading strategies can be identified in fixed income Treasuries issued (on-the-run), and the prices of the next to last Treasuries that have very similar maturity dates, will converge when the demand for on-the-run Treasuries slows down as a result of a new Treasury issue.
- Yield curve arbitrage: the fund manager expects changes in the slope of the various areas of a specific interest rate curve. One type of yield curve arbitrage is the so-called butterfly trade, whereby you open a position that has a relative value between a seven-year Treasury that is more expensive with respect to two Treasuries at six and eight years.
- Intermarket spread trading: the fund manager trades between two yield curves of different currencies.

- Futures basis trading (basis trading): the strategy of seeking to take advantage of mismatches between the price of a future contract and the price of the instruments to be delivered at contract expiration.
- Swap spread trading: the fund manager seeks to take advantage of changes in a particular swap spread, which is the difference between the fixed return a market participant is willing to pay to a counterparty in an interest rate swap and the yield of a Treasury having a similar duration.
- Other types of spread trade: for example, the spread between municipal bonds and Treasury bonds, whereby the fund manager seeks to take advantage of temporary deviations of the relationship observed between the prices of related financial instruments and the theoretical relationship existing between them.
- Capital structure arbitrage.
- Long/short credit or credit pair trading.
- Carry trade.
- Break-even inflation trade.
- Emerging markets fixed income.
- Cross-currency relative value trade.
- Treasuries over Eurodollar spread (international credit spread).
- Structured finance.
- Volatility trading: the manager seeks to profit from the difference between the current market opinion on volatility, observable in the implicit price volatility of an option, and the manager's expectations on future realized volatility.
- Mortgage trade: the fund manager seeks to profit from an apparent mispricing between mortgage instruments, mortgage derivatives and related financial instruments.

4.2.3 Mortgage-Backed Securities Arbitrage

A mortgage-backed security (MBS) is the securitization of a set of mortgages collateralized by real estate. Through MBS, the set of mortgages held by a financial institution is pooled and sold to investors. Like convertible bonds, MBSs are also hybrid securities that make an ideal arbitrage target for specialized hedge fund managers.

From an investor's perspective, an MBS is a fixed-income security embedding a prepayment option. Homeowners can choose to prepay all or part of their loan at any time throughout the entire mortgage. This option makes the mortgage's future cash flow, and therefore the value of the MBS, uncertain.

Traditional models are not suited to valuating the prepayment option embedded in an MBS. Specialized MBS arbitrageurs use proprietary models to estimate the present value of future MBS cash flows, i.e. to estimate the option-adjusted spread. The option-adjusted spread (OAS) of an MBS is the average spread above the yield curve of Treasury bonds, and makes the market price of an MBS equal to the estimate of the present value of future MBS cash flows. In other words, it is the security's incremental value with respect to Treasury bonds having a matching maturity, adjusted for the interest rate volatility and the impact of possible MBS prepayments. The higher the option-adjusted spread, the cheaper the MBS.

Mortgage-backed securities are, therefore, classified by option-adjusted spreads, and the MBSs that offer the highest OAS values are purchased and hedged with short sales of Treasury bonds of equal duration or with the sale of Treasury bond futures, to establish a position with zero duration – namely, a position hedged against the interest rate risk. As the spreads between the long and short positions are generally relatively small, hedge fund managers specializing in this strategy can use leverage, which exposes the fund manager to the risk that brokers might make a margin call, forcing the fund manager to liquidate some positions at unfavourable rates at the worst possible time. MBSs are, in fact, highly sensitive to Treasury yield curve shifts. MBS arbitrage strategies adopted by hedge funds can be classified on the basis of the different types of MBS on which fund managers decide to operate, as they display different characteristics in terms of risk, yield and liquidity.

Hedging MBSs by short selling Treasuries leaves the fund manager exposed to many risks, foremost of which is liquidity risk as the liquidity of Treasuries is better than the liquidity of the MBSs.

4.3 DIRECTIONAL TRADING

Directional/trading strategies seek to exploit big market tendencies rather than focus their analysis on single securities. In this section we focus on macro and managed futures strategies.

4.3.1 Global Macro

Global macro fund managers have the broadest investment mandate among the various types of existing hedge funds. Managers can invest in almost any market, using any financial instrument. Their investment approach is typically top-down, as their choices are prevailingly based on the analysis of macroeconomic variables associated with the different countries in which they have decided to allocate their capital. Econometric models generate market forecasts, trying to leverage the inconsistencies perceived by the statistical analysis of macroeconomic variables, such as:

- Gross domestic product;
- Trade balance;
- Current account balance;
- Public and private debt;
- CPI and PPI;
- Non-farm payrolls;
- Initial jobless claims;
- Slope of the yield curves;
- Exchange rates;
- Commodity prices;
- Housing market, etc.

Fund managers form their own view as to the prevailing trends on financial markets, and then try to capture returns by trading in the main world macroeconomic indices. They trade all asset classes (Treasuries, currencies, corporate bonds, precious metals, commodities), use all financial instruments (securities, indices, options, spot, forward and future contracts, swaps, etc.) and use short selling and leverage. Some invest in commodities only by way of derivatives, whereas others even invest in physical commodities. Generally, there are no predetermined geographical restrictions to their investments, therefore they can trade all over the world, from G10 countries to emerging markets.

Macro fund managers try to anticipate price changes on capital markets and often establish directional positions (i.e. not hedged). To identify events that will produce price changes, they focus on the analysis of how political events, global macroeconomic factors, economic and financial fundamentals and other external factors influence the valuation of financial instruments. At the same time, they also analyse capital markets directly, and the risk/return potential of a given investment.

If, through the top-down analysis of fundamentals, the fund manager decides to anticipate a market trend, he is going to use the financial market analysis to determine the market timing and the financial instruments that best suit his opinion. Every trading decision must necessarily be consistent with the manager's macroeconomic view, but it also has to be consistent with the risk profile of the entire portfolio. In addition, for global macro hedge funds, the main objective is capital preservation.

Due to the directional bias of their investments, global macro fund managers generally offer little transparency to their investors. They deny interviews to journalists, and if they discuss their performance with the investors at all it will be several months later, and in very general terms.

In the case of macro funds, however, the key player is the manager, who, with his insight and skill, generates investment ideas and seeks to seize the less obvious investment opportunities. Profits will be reaped if the fund manager correctly anticipates the price movements on global financial markets. Their investment philosophy is opportunistic, as they trade in any capital market sector presenting profit opportunities, and with any financial instrument, in that they opportunistically replicate the most specialized strategies belonging to the other fund classes. Macro funds are similar to multi-strategy funds, except that they carry out directional investments and many discretionary hedge funds are very similar to managed futures funds.

In comparison to the hedge funds managed along the strategies previously analysed, global macro hedge funds are generally characterized by a larger size in terms of assets under management. Directional strategies represent a substantial departure from the original hedge fund philosophy according to the Alfred Winslow Jones model. In broad terms, macro funds are also defined as being hedge funds, not because they provide a hedge, but because they are not subject to the constraints and limitations of mutual investment funds. Instead of hedging market risks, they seek to profit from the direction of movements on financial markets, establishing directional positions that reflect their predictions in terms of market direction. As a result, their performance fully depends on the quality and timing of their predictions.

4.3.2   Managed Futures (CTA or Systematic Futures Trading)

A futures contract is a standardized agreement between two parties to buy or sell a specific amount of a commodity (raw materials, agricultural produces) or a financial instrument (shares, interest rates, indices or currencies) at a particular price on a stipulated future date. However, the amount actually exchanged between the parties is not the amount of the assets underlying the futures contract, but is instead the margin. The margin of a futures contract is the amount of money a hedge fund deposits with a broker to start a trade on a futures contract and keep open positions on futures contracts. The managed futures strategy (often inappropriately called CTA, from the name of the type of management company adopting it, i.e. the Commodity Trading Advisors) is similar to the macro strategy, since both are directional strategies investing prevailingly in futures listed worldwide. The primary difference is that in the managed futures strategy the fund manager's emotions are eclipsed by the use of computerized models that automatically make trading decisions. The fund manager can only periodically readjust the trading model parameters.

CTAs develop many models that are processed by a computer in real time in order to pick a trend in each of more than 100 different futures markets and on different time horizons. They follow the trend until it expires, first with a back-test on historical data, then with the management of a test portfolio, and finally with the management of true data in real time. A good trading system must minimize the brokerage fees paid by the fund, minimize volatility and minimize slippage, which curbs the strategy's profitability. In fact, overly intensive trading may accumulate high brokerage fees that negatively affect performance.

Risk management is very important and, for this reason, sophisticated risk management systems are put in place. For example, losing positions are gradually reduced through stop loss techniques, net market exposure is limited, or the fund manager tries to increase positions that are inversely correlated with those that are reporting a loss. Some fund managers link the position's size with its volatility. Pattern recognition systems seek to identify market trends on different time horizons, i.e. to spot whether a weekly trend is forming on soybean futures, a fortnightly trend on oil futures, or a 3-hour trend on NASDAQ futures. Back-testing is often misleading, as it is relatively easy to find a model that suits the historical data.

Managed futures can be concentrated in a limited number of positions or can offer a diversification on a wide variety of futures markets:

- Equities
- Bonds
- Shrot term interest rates
- Currencies
- Energies
- Metals
- Agriculturals.

If trading in range or sideways markets, managed futures that follow medium to long-term periods are at a disadvantage, as there is no trend to profit from. Classical trend-following models are also at a disadvantage when a medium to long-term trend suddenly shifts direction, because they can recognize the reversal of a main trend only after a certain delay.

In order to assess the solvency of a managed futures fund it is important to verify its margin-to-equity, which is the existing ratio between the margins put up as a guarantee to the futures contracts and the hedge fund's net equity. Generally, a high leverage is used.

CTAs also differ from other strategies in terms of length of time horizon, which is the frequency of moves they try to follow: long-term trends are those lasting from 1 to 6 months, medium-term trends are those lasting 8 to 30 days and short-term trends last from 1 to 7 days. Short-term trend followers specialize in the analysis of the market microstructure and the price formation mechanism, and try to identify the fastest trends. They will enter a position immediately after the first strong movement that follows a trend reversal. This will lead to a high frequency of deals with limited gains or losses and often with an incidence of high trading costs. Long-term trend followers try to identify the slowest trends; they will ride a trend while it is developing and will need generally more time to identify a trend reversal. As a result, they will carry out less trade with respect to short trend followers, and will make greater gains or losses.

The weight invested on the different markets can change depending on opportunities. Managed futures trade very liquid instruments and long and short positions can be established very easily through the purchase or sale of futures. Valuating the portfolio is simple because practically it is no more than assigning market price to the futures present in the portfolio. The high liquidity of futures contracts allows managed futures funds to offer good settlement conditions to investors (daily, weekly or fortnightly liquidity).

Besides the typical risk monitoring indicators, there are two specific indicators to monitor the behaviour of these programmes:

- Margin to equity;
- Roundturn[1] per year per million.

---

[1] Roundturn is the number of times one million dollar turns (or is traded) every year.

4.4   EVENT-DRIVEN (OR SPECIAL SITUATION)

The event-driven investment strategy, also called special situations, refers to opportunities that arise throughout a company's life and that are created by extraordinary, or special, corporate events, such as:

- Spin-offs;
- Mergers;
- Acquisitions;
- Business consolidations;
- Liquidations;
- Reorganizations;
- Bankruptcies;
- Recapitalizations;
- Share buy-backs;
- Hostile takeover bids;
- Changes in benchmark or index composition;
- Sale or purchase of assets;
- Discrepancies in the value of share classes;
- Agreements;
- Legal disputes;
- Investments in real assets.

So-called special situations are characterized by catalytic events, i.e. events that can drive the price towards a new value.

Depending on the opportunities available on the market, fund managers dynamically allocate their capital across the different sub-strategies. The event-driven strategy consists in trying to predict the outcome of a given deal, as well as the best time to allocate capital in the investment. The uncertainty surrounding the outcome of these events creates investment opportunities for those fund managers who are correct in assessing the outcome and timing of these complex situations in advance. The event-driven strategy also includes other strategies, such as merger arbitrage and distressed securities.

4.4.1   Merger Arbitrage

The merger arbitrage strategy seeks to seize opportunities arising from extraordinary corporate events, such as mergers and acquisitions (M&A) or leveraged buy-outs, by trading the stocks of the companies involved in the deal. In general, in these transactions common stock is exchanged for cash, other common stock, or a combination of cash and stocks. The merger arbitrage strategy is more properly called risk arbitrage, because it is an arbitrage strategy whose outcome purely depends on the risk associated with the outcome of the deal. Its success totally depends on the finalization of the mergers and acquisitions. The hedge fund manager takes a directional position on the spread:

- In the case of acquisition, the manager takes a position between the value offered for the acquisition and the current market value of the company to be acquired.
- In the case of a merger, the manager takes a position between the theoretical exchange ratio of the stock of the two merging entities and the exchange ratio currently expressed by the market.

The greater the risk of a deal failing, the greater is the spread. All mergers/acquisitions are exposed to the risk that the deal is not closed as announced initially.

If the deal fails, generally the value of the target company's shares drop sharply. The hedge fund manager opens arbitrage positions on mergers and acquisitions where he expects the current market spread to converge towards the offered spread. The manager will make a profit if the spread narrows, and will lose money if the spread widens. He can choose between two approaches: take a position after the transaction has been announced; or try to anticipate the merger or acquisition event and take a position before the announcement. Generally, hedge fund managers trade after the deal has been announced. To invest in anticipation of an event means that the investment is made on rumours or, which is even worse, on confidential information, which translates into the illegal practice of insider trading.

4.4.2 Distressed Securities

The distressed securities market has been a rather obscure area in the last 20 years, and has only recently been under the spotlight of the press due to the Enron, Adelphia, WorldCom and Parmalat scandals. Certainly, the fact that distressed securities trade mainly over-the-counter contributed towards building this image.

There are many different opinions on what to include under distressed securities, and one should always be wary of what a fund manager actually implies when he uses this definition. In general, distressed securities are shares, bonds trade receivables or financial loans of companies on the verge of, in the middle of, or emerging from, bankruptcy or financial distress. The quality of any bond is based on the issuer's financial ability to oblige payments of interest and return the full principal when due. Rating services help with assessing the creditworthiness of bonds, and are a good indicator of the quality of one issuer compared to others.

We can identify four types of distressed securities depending on the situation of the issuer:

- Pre-reorganization securities: securities of companies that are entering restructuring and where it is easy to sell the company's securities short. The risk profile is high, but the risk premium is sizeable.
- Interim-reorganization securities: securities of companies that are complying with the restructuring plan. A wide range of investors holds the new debt securities and the liquidity of the securities is good. The reorganization process can lead to the issue of orphan shares.
- Mature distressed: the reorganization plan is operational and the securities of the restructured company start to reflect the company's improved health conditions.
- Deeply distressed: the defaulting company is wound up and distressed securities trade at a discount to the company's recovery rate, also under the worst scenario. It is possible to identify inexpensive options on potentially positive events, such as higher

recovery values or a lower number of legal actions and liabilities than expected.

Besides the debtor's insolvency, the characteristics shared by all these securities are their illiquidity, which can be caused for different reasons:

- Delisting: in most cases, companies filing for bankruptcy under Chapter 11 of the US Bankruptcy Code are generally unable to meet the listing requirements to continue to be traded on the NASDAQ or the New York Stock Exchange. Hence, they are delisted from these major stock exchanges. Since there is no federal law prohibiting the trading of shares of a bankruptcy company, their shares can continue to be traded either on the over-the-counter (OTC) market or on Pink Sheets.
- Legal constraints: many institutional investors cannot buy distressed securities because their articles of association, their fiduciary responsibilities or their regulatory authorities forbid them to hold speculative grade securities, even though the issuer can generate profits.
- Lack of coverage by analysts: coverage by analysts tends to decline significantly when a company is under distress, until it almost disappears in the case of bankruptcy. Clearly, the low interest by investors and the specific nature of the bankruptcy procedures erode the incentive for equity analysts to devote time collecting and analysing information. A lack of information, in turn, generates low interest by investors.
- Lack of knowledge: the valuation of distressed securities requires a lot of work and several skills, together with constant access to the latest information on issuers. Creditors often prefer to sell their securities at a strongly discounted price, because they do not have the knowledge, the interest, the skills or the time to conduct the necessary analyses.

This situation results in a disorganized and illiquid distressed securities market that does not have a solid offer price structure. Most orders are on the sale-side, with traditional investors unwilling to buy. This allows hedge funds to inject liquidity into the market and profit from its inability to appreciate the intrinsic value of these securities.

Hedge funds that are managed along a distressed securities strategy have a net long position on distressed securities, or, in other words, they have a long bias. This characteristic exposes distressed securities' hedge funds to the risk of credit spread widening, which by driving prices down would cause them to report a negative performance. An additional relevant risk associated with investments in distressed securities is the liquidity risk. Typically, distressed securities' hedge funds have a quarterly, 6-monthly or annual liquidity due to the illiquidity of the securities and the long time horizons to finalize the manager's strategy. Finally, there is the problem of the valuation of distressed securities: in the absence of trades, prices do not change and are often based on a purely accounting reckoning. Hence, investors must make sure that the portfolio of distressed securities is valued by an independent administrator, who prices the securities on the basis of criteria that must not change over time.

4.5 OTHER STRATEGIES

Among the strategies not included in the previous categories, the most common and theoretically relevant are:

- Statistical arbitrage;
- Index arbitrage;
- Volatility arbitrage;
- Multi-strategy.

4.5.1 Statistical Arbitrage

This strategy seeks to capture imbalances in expected values of financial instruments, while trying to be market-neutral. Typically, the said imbalances stem from the segmentation of the financial instrument market and the specialization of market operators in a single segment. The identification process of a trading opportunity starts by estimating the theoretical value of thousands of financial instruments, using the current price flow downloaded from information providers and the hedge fund's database containing historical data. The quantitative analysis process continues with the analysis of the difference between the theoretical value and the market current value. Considering a specific stock, the possible pricing abnormality can be confronted with historical data or with similar financial instruments. The divergence between the theoretical value and the market value of a given financial instrument does not imply by itself a prediction of future price movements, therefore it does not imply a profit opportunity. There could, for example, be an explanation in some market dynamics, such as fiscal reasons, economic reasons, the desire by some investors to replicate an index, etc. This is why it is important for the fund manager to carry out a qualitative analysis when assessing potential investment opportunities. Arbitrage opportunities are the outcome of a quantitative filtering process and a qualitative evaluation process. Fund managers use proprietary mathematical processes to analyse thousands of financial instruments in a wide range of asset classes and countries in search of potential abnormalities in market valuations. In-house research analysts construct databases that they keep updated with historical financial data of various kinds that are accessible by all company employees. Pricing abnormalities are typically identified through an assumption formulation, testing, and a rigorous validation process. Valuation abnormalities that prove statistically significant are then used in trading strategies, which typically operate in real time based on an almost continuous flow of financial data fed by Bloomberg, Reuters and other information providers. The identification of multiple market pricing abnormalities is very difficult: it takes time and is expensive. Experimental results are then used to refine the adopted models. Optimization software products help to construct and dynamically change the portfolio makeup, with the aim of maximizing the portfolio's expected return, minimizing risk, controlling the portfolio's liquidity and minimizing transaction costs.

4.5.2 Index Arbitrage

This strategy seeks to profit from the spread convergence between a futures contract and its basket of securities. If the fund manager believes that the spread is going to narrow down, he will simultaneously buy a basket of securities having the exact weight as that in the futures contract and sell the futures contract short. He will do the opposite if he believes that the spread is going to widen. Fund managers specializing in this type of arbitrage actively trade on the days that index changes have been announced, when there are securities entering and exiting indices. A classical strategy is the purchase of a security that has to be added to the index and the concurrent sale of an equal amount of futures on the index to hedge the position against market risk. This deal is based on the observation that passive funds rebalance their positions on the day in which the index is actually changed.

4.5.3 Volatility Arbitrage

Volatility arbitrage is a strategy whereby the hedge fund manager seeks to profit from volatility changes, without being affected by the direction of the price movement. In volatility trading, fund managers trade on derivatives – such as options, warrants and futures – on securities of a single issuer as well as on market indices. The fund manager can go long or short the volatility depending on the expected changes in the volatility of the underlying security, as well as on changes in implied volatility. Volatility can be considered as the most intuitive and basic – but undoubtedly not the only – form of measuring risk when investing in a financial asset. Volatility trades are now easier to execute than in the past, due to new risk management technologies, easier access to financial information and the introduction of listed and unlisted dedicated products, which allow investors to express their view on volatility more rapidly and easily. Volatility traders are typically looking for options that misprice volatility. In fact, volatility is one of the main factors affecting option prices.

By delta hedging and trading options, it is possible to take a directional position on the fact that the realized volatility will be higher or lower than the implied volatility. It is also possible to open a position on the basis that the implied volatility may rise or fall. This can be done by trading a combination of listed options. In recent years, brokers have introduced *over-the-counter* products, including forward-starting options and forward-starting variance swaps, which allow investors to express their views on volatility in a more simple and rapid way. The growing interest devoted to these products contributed to the development of pure volatility products. The most popular is the VXO Futures Contract traded at the CBOE, which allows investors to express their view on the volatility of the S&P 500 index.

4.5.4 Multi-Strategy

Multi-strategy funds generally specialize in convertible bond arbitrage, fixed income arbitrage, distressed securities, event-driven and merger arbitrage. Depending on the opportunities offered by the markets, the fund manager decides which percentage of his capital he intends to allocate to the single strategies, and in this way the fund manager can seek to capture multiple opportunities, without having to invest along a specific strategy that, in given market circumstances, could prove unprofitable. Another advantage brought by multi-strategy funds is the diversification of return sources across multiple strategies.

Generally, the front offices of the management companies of multi-strategy hedge funds are organized into trading groups, each specializing in a specific investment strategy. The hedge fund's chief investment officer is the person deciding the hedge fund's capital allocation across the various trading groups, and he changes this allocation dynamically depending on the opportunities that he predicts will be presented by single strategies. Multi-strategy funds are similar to global macro funds from the point of view of the fund manager's discretionary powers in allocating capital across the various strategies, but they differ in terms of lack of investment directionality. Sometimes they also share with global macro funds the large size of the assets under management and the organizational structure of the management company.

4.6   LIMITS IMPOSED BY UCITS III

4.6.1   Considerations

When considering the creation of a UCITS fund, the strategy pursued by the target fund must necessarily be analysed in the context of the UCITS rules. While UCITS III provides more possibilities concerning the products and leverage employed in a strategy, there are also some constraints that the strategy has to fulfil.

4.6.2   Background

The UCITS directive was introduced in 1985 with the aim of creating a uniform regulatory framework concerning the distribution of open-ended funds, investing in non-proprietary assets within the EU. The first version of the directive underwent a change during the 1990s, since different barriers to the cross-borders marketing of funds had prevented its success. The second version of the directive was considered to be too ambitious, and was soon abandoned by the European Cabinet. The third and current UCITS version was submitted to the European Commission in 1998. The proposal was composed of two parts: a "Management Directive" and a "Product Directive", which were subsequently adopted and now form the fundamental set up of the UCITS. The "Management Directive", in particular, allows a "European passport" to be granted to the funds that meet the necessary requirements. The "Product Directive", on the other hand, defines the financial products that can be used to pursue investment strategies.

4.6.3   Characteristics of the UCITS III Funds Appreciated by Investors

An ever-increasing number of investors have shown an interest in the UCITS III versions of the alternative investment funds for the following reasons:

- Liquidity: in most unfavourable cases, the UCITS III fund must guarantee 2 months liquidity. In any case, the largest part of these funds provide a weekly liquidity, if not daily.

- Asset safety: physical assets are held in custody with no remortgage rights. Leverage and short sale are allowed, but must be implemented through derivatives, usually swaps.
- Higher diversification: there are particularly strict limits to exposure towards single issuers.
- Risk management process: the process is checked by the vigilance authorities.
- Transparency: approval of the fund prospectus and risk manual, in addition to an annual or half-year report to investors.
- Regulated product: many investors may not have had previous access to alternative investment strategies in structures of offshore funds. In this case, the regulation to which the products are subject provides a further guarantee, as well as higher control levels.

4.6.4   Main UCITS Rules

- Exposure towards a single issuer: it is not possible to invest more than 10% of NAV in non-proprietary assets of the same issuer.
- 5/10/40 rule: the total value of the concentrated exposures in a single issuer that comprises between 5% and 10% of NAV cannot exceed 40% of NAV.
- Concentration rules: the fund, or division, cannot buy shares that include a single issuer's voting rights or allow a significant influence to be exercised on the management of the same issuer. This limitation is set up to 20% of the shares with voting rights. Furthermore, the fund or division cannot own:
  - more than 10% of shares without the voting rights of the same issuer;
  - more than 10% of the debt securities of the same issuer;
  - more than 25% of the shares of the same UCITS and/or other UCIs;
  - more than 10% of currency market instruments of any other issuer.
- No short sales of physical assets or share lending: the short exposure must be obtained by using derivatives. For instance, the short exposure on equity can be obtained through swaps. This kind

of regulation could make additional OTC counterparties necessary. The number of counterparties and the operational resources
necessary to manage these relations should be considered.

- Regulated markets: the portfolio should be composed of non-
  proprietary assets or derivative instruments traded on regulated
  markets, as defined in the ISD directive.
- Liquidity: the portfolio must be sufficiently liquid in order to meet
  the potential requirements of weekly settlements. Weak liquid positions are allowed, as long as such positions do not represent the
  main fund strategy.
- If the fund is declared "sophisticated", then the portfolio risk is
  measured using a VAR-type approach and it is possible to obtain
  a higher leverage as long as VAR limits are satisfied.
- Leverage: if a fund is declared "non-sophisticated", the maximum
  leverage permitted is 200% of NAV if on the fund's domicile.
  For instance, the Luxembourg limit is set as an absolute VAR
  of 20%, based on a 99% confidence level, with a holding period of 20 working days, using a historical series of at least one
  year.
- Replicable indices: all indices must meet the following requirements:
  – they must be sufficiently diversified; all securities must represent
    less than 35% of the index and none of the other securities can
    exceed 20% of the index;
  – they must represent an adequate benchmark for the reference
    market;
  – they must be published in a proper way;
  – small diversified indices can be traded by the division as long as
    these indices are used for purposes of diversification and do not
    exceed 49% of the fund's gross exposure.
- Exposure on treasuries: exposure towards Treasury bonds of a
  single issuer is limited to 35% of NAV. This limit can be passed as
  long as:
  – less than 30% of NAV is composed of a single issue;
  – the fund owns at least six different issues;

– the aim is to make compensation between different issues in order to comply with the limit of 30%; for instance, it is allowed to be 70% long on a 10-year bond and 40% short on a 5-year bond.

4.6.5   Additional Rules to Consider

- Exposure towards OTC counterparties: exposure limit towards a single counterparty is equal to 10% of NAV in the case of a bank, and 5% of NAV otherwise;
- Deposits: not more than 20% of NAV can be deposited in a single bank;
- Coverage rules: the fund must own liquid assets sufficient to meet the requirements coming from derivative instruments held in the portfolio;
- New issues: any new issue bought by the fund must have been listed for at least one year and this documentation must be included in the prospectus;
- Trash ratio: non-proprietary assets listed on non-regulated markets can represent not more than 10% of NAV.

4.6.6   Collateral Management Guidelines

The fund can use loans of securities through repo or reverse repo transactions, as long as these transactions are made with the aim of an efficient portfolio management and meet the following requirements:

- They are cost-effective.
- Their aim is to reduce portfolio risk or management costs.
- Their risk is considered in the risk management process of the fund.

Repo or reverse repo transactions can be performed only towards these kinds of collateral:

- Short-term bank certificates or currency market instruments;
- Bonds issued or guaranteed by an OECD Member State, by local authorities or supranational agencies;
- UCI shares, as long as their NAV is calculated on a daily basis and their rating is equal to AAA or equivalent;

- Bonds issued by non-governmental agencies, offering an adequate liquidity level;
- Shares listed or traded in an EU Member State's regulated market or in a stock exchange of an OECD Member State, on condition that these shares are included in an index.

Any share loan must be guaranteed for an amount at least equal to 90% of the asset value, and this guarantee must be one of the following:

- Liquid assets that can include a letter of credit or a guarantee provided by first-class banks.
- Bonds issued or guaranteed by an OECD Member State, by its authorities or supranational agencies.
- Shares issued by UCI, as long as their NAV is calculated on a daily basis and their rating is equal to AAA or equivalent.
- UCITS shares mainly investing in bond or shares defined in the following two points;
- Bonds issued by non governmental agencies offering an adequate liquidity level;
- Shares listed or traded in an EU Member State's regulated market or in a stock exchange of an OECD Member State, on condition that these shares are included in an index.

4.7 "SYNTHETIC" SHORT SELLING AND CONTRACTS FOR DIFFERENCE

According to Article 42 of the 85/611/CEE directive, neither the investment company nor the management company nor the depositary (on behalf of the common investment funds) is authorized to short sell non-proprietary assets, currency market instruments or other financial instruments.

However, as UCITS may invest in derivative instruments, it is permissible to indirectly create synthetic-type short positions by using the so-called contract for difference (CFD). The CFD is a swap subscribed as a contract between two parties in which the acquirer, against the payment of an interest rate (usually Euribor or Libor, plus a spread), receives the return of an underlying financial asset, while the seller, against this interest, commits himself to payment of the return of the underlying asset.

The acquirer and the seller then sign an agreement to exchange the financial flow deriving from the price difference between the underlying financial asset at the opening of the contract and the same asset at its expiry. (Revenues and losses resulting from these differences are then multiplied by the number of traded CFDs.) Then, in order to short sell a financial security it is sufficient to assume a short CFD position on that underlying. Despite the fact that the negotiation of CFD occurs in a similar manner to other financial instruments, it is not necessary in this type of contract to pay the whole value of the transaction, since only a marginal deposit is required. This margin generally varies from 10% to 20% of the total value of the underlying asset. In addition to being able to replicate short positions, this instrument allows the client to invest in leverage (obviously, the leverage negatively depends on the amount required as margin).

4.8 SYNTHETIC NEWCITS

This last section of the chapter discusses a new trend recently developed: Newcits funds with a single total return swap (TRS) on a financial index as underlying. Some high profile hedge fund managers have launched synthetic Newcits funds implementing systematic trading futures or event driven strategies that otherwise could not be implemented inside a UCITS compliant fund.

Figure 4.1 overleaf shows an example of the structure of a synthetic Newcits.

The process can be simplified as follows:

1. The investor subscribes into the Newcits fund and receives the fund's units, or shares;
2. The Newcits fund transfers the issuance proceeds to the Index Sponsor and signs a TRS agreement, in order to receive the Index performance;

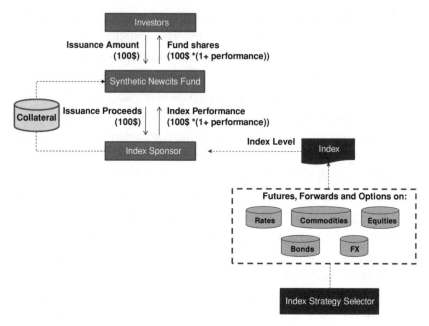

Figure 4.1 Example of structure of a Synthetic Newcits

3. The Index Sponsor posts eligible UCITS financial instruments (e.g. AAA Government bonds) as collateral to the Newcits fund to mitigate counterparty risk;
4. In order to hedge itself, the Index Sponsor invests in the offshore fund or in an offshore managed account;
5. The Index Sponsor and the Newcits fund regulate the TRS contract:
   a. The Newcits fund, acting as Protection Seller, or Total Return Receiver, must pay an amount that is equal to the EURIBOR (or similar inter-bank interest rate) + the TRS spread (either positive or negative);
   b. The Index Sponsor, acting as Protection Buyer, or Total Return Payer, must pay an amount that is equal to the performance of the Index;
   c. Only the net cash flow of this operation is exchanged: if positive, the Index Sponsor pays the Newcits fund; if negative,

the Index Sponsor charges off the amount from the collateral posted to the fund;

d. At the expiration of the TRS contract, the collateral is also settled;

6. The Investor receives the performance of the Newcits fund.

The tracking error between the Newcits fund and the offshore hedge fund that it aims to replicate is generated by:

1. different fee structure: management fees and performance fees paid by the Newcits fund to the Index Sponsor (index administration and replication fees, collateral fee, etc...), management fees and performance fees paid by the Index Sponsor to the Index Strategy Selector, plus other fixed fees, taxe d'abonnement, currency conversion fees, etc;
2. different frequency of subscriptions and redemptions: the Newcits fund has daily or weekly or bi-monthly liquidity while the offshore hedge fund has monthly or quarterly liquidity;
3. different cash management policies: this is important especially in the case of systematic futures trading strategies where the level of unencumbered cash is usually between 80% and 90%;
4. the index has a limit not to invest more than 35% in securities issued by the same body while the offshore funds are practically unconstrained.

The only rule regulating investment aiming at the replication of a certain index, is contained in art. 22a of Council Directive 85/611/EEC). This rule sets to a maximum of 20% the investment in shares and/or debt securities issued by the same body. This limit can be raised, by a Member State, to a maximum of 35% where it is justified by exceptional market conditions. No specific rule compels the managers to aggregate index components on the basis of correlation, although practitioners often consider securities with a correlation higher than 80% as a single asset.

In our opinion, synthetic Newcits might frustrate the spirit of the UCITS III directive, even if regulators authorize them. Sometimes, their structures are so complex that institutional investors need to conduct an in-depth due diligence in order to be sufficiently aware of the risks and the drawbacks of these products. In one case, for instance, the complexities of both the total return swap and its legal documentation was so high that the administrator had to restate the fund's NAV for several months.

Even though this solution has been allowed by regulators, in our opinion it raises both new opportunities and risks. In fact, due to the complexities of these structures, the eventual impact of tracking error is not completely quantifiable to the investor in the moment of the subscription.

In particular, the swap replication approach might go against the principle of fund management transparency (which is one of the main pillars of the UCITS III directive) because:

1. the structure bears additional fees: management expenses of the collateral, TRS additional negative cash flows (EURIBOR or LIBOR + TRS spread) + currency conversion fees (for instance, when the fund units are denominated in EUR but the Index Sponsor invests in USD);
2. the TRS can be not fully collateralized (i.e. less than 100%) increasing the counterparty risk;
3. the structure bears additional risks: management of the collateral, multiple counterparty risks;
4. there is a conflict of interest because the swap provider is often the fund sponsor;
5. the terms of the total return swap are contained in the ISDA agreement plus or the Credit Support Annex or the Credit Support Deed but they are usually not disclosed to final investors;
6. it is not always clear if the collateral is in the balance sheet of the fund (i.e. collateral can be "pledged") or in the balance sheet of the swap provider;
7. it is not always clear the extent to which the custodian bank of the fund can exercise control of the posted collateral.

5

The Early Stages of the Newcits Industry[1]

In recent months many investment companies have launched a UCITS III version of their hedge funds and many others are preparing to do so in the near future. It is therefore necessary to immediately pursue a quantitative research on the world, still very unexplored, of the Newcits funds. These products have certainly great potential, at least when we consider the interest they have generated for the final investors. However, it is only when they have attained a certain degree of efficiency – especially in terms of assets under management and the number of products on the market – can we say whether the "double-edged weapon" of greater liquidity and transparency will be able to offer investors the performance levels that the operational flexibility and the breadth of hedge strategies have shown.

5.1 DESCRIPTION OF SAMPLE

The data collected on the market of the Newcits helps to identify common traits and distinctive characteristics of this new phenomenon in the asset management industry. According to our calculations, at 30 June 2010 there are 416 Newcits funds that have raised nearly €51.8 billion of assets under management (excluding flexible funds, replicas of hedge funds and products of tactical asset allocation). The growing interest of the management companies in these products has given rise to an exponential increase in the number of Newcits, registering a compound annual growth rate of around 21.27%

[1]The authors thank Fabio Cividini, graduate student at the University of Bergamo, Faculty of Engineering, for the superb research assistance in this chapter. All errors are due to the authors.

number of funds

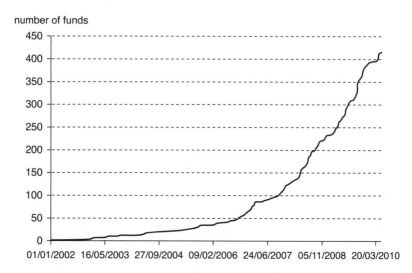

Figure 5.1 Newcits funds launched since the directive become effective

since the UCITS III directive became effective on December 2001
(Figure 5.1).

The Newcits market is still at an early stage – evidenced by the
fact that as many as 66.7% of the sample individually manage assets
to the tune of less than or equal to €100 million, and only 4.4%
have assets under management exceeding €900 million. The curve
in Figure 5.2 shows the concentration in the Newcits market, where
we note that from the sample of 273 funds that reported AUM data on
Bloomberg, the top 18 funds, equivalent to 6.6% of the total, handles
about 50% of AUM, and the first 61, equivalent to 22% of the total,
manages 80%.

An analysis of the types of funds used (Figure 5.3) shows how the
majority of funds have the corporate designation of SICAV (77%),
followed by those of FCP (13%), OEIC (8%) and Unit Trust (2%).
The difference between the corporate designations of SICAV and
FCP, and the British equivalent OEIC and Unit Trust, depends exclusively on the jurisdiction of the country in which the fund is
domiciled. The domicile for 61% of cases is Luxembourg, followed
by France and Ireland, with 18% and 12% respectively. The final

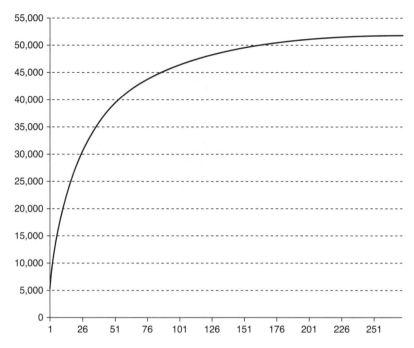

Figure 5.2   Newcits industry concentration curve on 30 June 2010 (€ million)

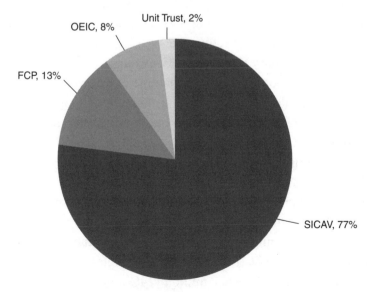

Figure 5.3   Types of Newcits funds

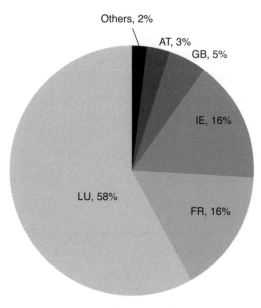

Figure 5.4   The domicile of Newcits funds

groups are domiciled in the United Kingdom (4%) and Austria (3%), followed by Finland, Germany, Italy and Sweden which, together, represent 2% of the total (Figure 5.4). This heterogeneity is mainly due to fiscal reasons, reflecting the type of tax system on funds adopted by the country of domicile. For example, Luxembourg provides for payment of taxes only at the time of disinvestment (i.e. on the realized), while Italy requires funds to make daily provisions for taxes and applies taxes on potential gains even if the investor does not cash in profits.

An important feature revealed by this investigation, and shown in Figure 5.5 is related to the liquidity of UCITS III compliant funds: daily in 73% of cases, while weekly and bi-monthly, respectively, for 17% and 10% of the funds.

As for the minimum initial investment for institutional investors, classes occurring most frequently are the single share of the fund (18%) and 500,000 (18%), 1 million (14%) and 10 million (11%) units of currency. With regard to retail investors, the individual share

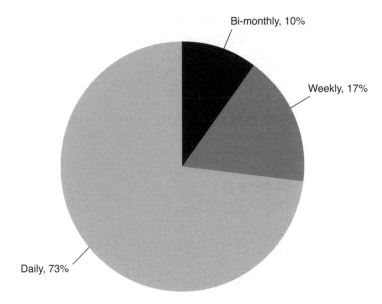

Figure 5.5 Liquidity of Newcits funds

of the fund is required in 39% of cases, followed by the classes of 1,000 (14%) and 5,000 (18%) units of currency.

5.2 IMPLEMENTED STRATEGIES

One limitation of Newcits products lies in the reduced range of strategies implemented compared with offshore hedge funds. As these strategies must adhere to the strict liquidity limits of the underlying imposed by the directive, the offshore hedge funds therefore remain unique, being able to focus on strategies that are characterized by different liquidity conditions from those used by the onshore managers of UCITS III products. Consequently, the strategies used by onshore managers are precisely those whose underlying liquidity is compatible with the parameters of the directive: i.e. long/short equity (26%), equity market neutral (17%) and multi-strategy (11%), as shown in Figure 5.6.

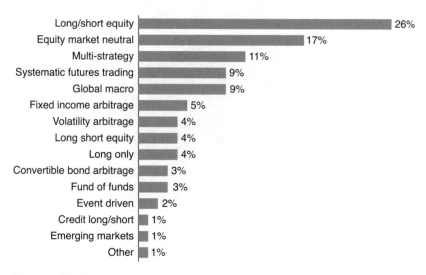

Figure 5.6 Implemented strategies

5.3 FEE STRUCTURE

Another peculiarity of Newcits funds should be the lower commission charges compared to those for traditional hedge funds. In fact, what emerges from this survey relative to performance fees is that 60% of the sample has a commission of 20%, while 12% apply other rates (Figure 5.7). In general, the principle of the High Watermark is applied when estimating the performance fee. This is a principle which states that the performance fee is only applied if the value of the NAV exceeds its historical maximum. This level is equal to the NAV for which the previous performance fee was paid, or to the NAV in which the class was launched if a performance fee has never been paid. Besides, the Hurdle Rate is expected in 82% of the products.

Regarding the structure of management fees, the average applied to institutional investors is approximately 1.1%, less than 40 basis points compared to the average commission applied to retail investors. Moreover, the management fee for 99% of institutional classes and

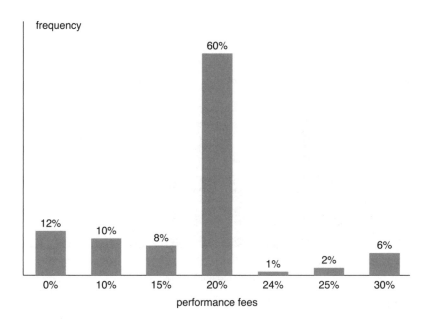

Figure 5.7 Performance fees

88% of retail classes does not exceed 2%, while (within 1%) shares decrease respectively at 62% and 23% of the sample (Figure 5.8).

5.4 PERFORMANCE ANALYSIS

Being a phenomenon of recent interest, and given the strong development of its new products in the latter period (some Newcits funds were launched almost every day in the first 6 months of 2010), the short time series only allows a comparison over short time intervals. The products born in 2009 were not taken into account in the year-to-date evaluation of product performance in order to use the series for as long a time as possible (and therefore more representative) on time horizons that were still homogeneous. In most cases, the performance of hedge funds are not GIPS® compliant. In particular, we have hedge funds with "Equalization factors", "Depreciation deposits" but more often hedge funds with classes and series that

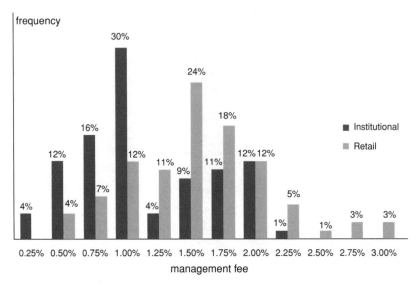

Figure 5.8 Performance fees for institutional and retail share classes

have slightly different performances. The reason for this complexity comes from performance fees calculated by the High Watermark method, where performance is dependent on the customer's date of entry. For simplicity, we considered the performances of the main classes of funds.

The average performance of the sample in 2009 (consisting of 159 funds) was equal to 12.0% with a volatility of 25.9%. The sample also shows that 41% of the products had a positive year-to-date performance between 10% and 6%, but not less negative than –5%, which applied to only 5% of the sample. Note also that a performance of over 100% was achieved by 3% of the products. Figure 5.9 shows the frequency distribution of these returns.

In the first 6 months of 2010, the average performance of the sample (consisting of 380 funds) is equal to –0.9% with a volatility of 5%. The sample also shows that 43% of the products had a positive year-to-date performance of which 41% were between 10% and 0%. Moreover, 15% of the sample were under –5%. Note also that no product achieved a performance above 20%. Figure 5.10 shows the frequency distribution of these returns.

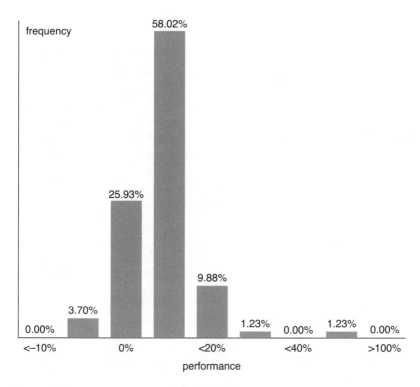

Figure 5.9 Performances of the sample in 2009

5.5 TRACKING ERROR AND TRACKING ERROR VOLATILITY

Calculating and monitoring the tracking error and its volatility allows us to study the repeatability of the offshore hedge funds in the Newcits vehicles.

The tracking error is calculated as the difference between the return obtained from the two types of funds in the same period. We define the market value of a hedge fund by the letter H and the value of the corresponding Newcits version by the letter U. We use R_H and R_U to identify their respective returns on a defined time frame:

$$R_H = \frac{\Delta H}{H} e \, R_U = \frac{\Delta U}{U}$$

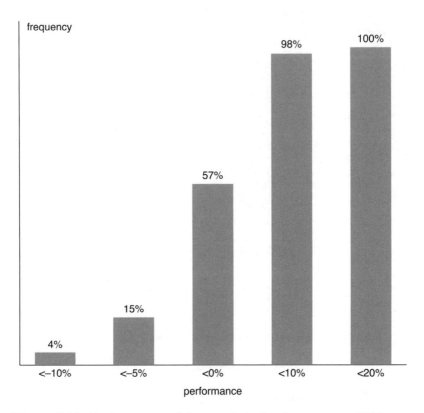

Figure 5.10   Performances of the sample in the first semester 2010

Now we can define the tracking error as:

$$TE = R_H - R_U$$

The standard deviation of the tracking error, or tracking error volatility (TEV), is given by:

$$TEV = \sigma_{(R_H - R_U)} = \sqrt{\sigma_H^2 - 2\rho_{H,U}\sigma_H\sigma_U + \sigma_U^2}$$

where $\rho_{H,U}$ is the correlation between the hedge fund's returns and the return of the Newcits product, while σ_H and σ_U are their respective volatilities. It is clear that a Newcits product is much more efficient if the average tracking error and tracking error volatility are close to zero.

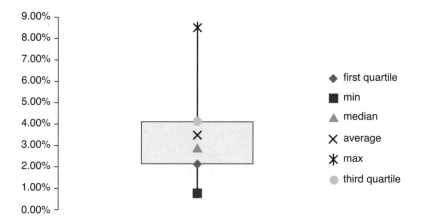

Figure 5.11 Box plot of tracking error volatility, sample of offshore hedge funds and corresponding Newcits

The results of the quantitative study conducted on a sample of offshore hedge funds, and the corresponding Newcits replicas, returned an annualized average tracking error volatility of 3.50% (Figure 5.11). In itself, the data is relatively weak, although we correlate it with the target volatility of the funds. However, it shows two outliers with a very high TEV of more than 8%.

These results are in line with expectations, taking into account that offshore Newcits funds suffer more limited operational flexibility compared to onshore hedge funds due to:

- more frequent subscription and redemption flows;
- management fees, performance and other costs;
- more stringent limits on risk diversification;
- limits on asset classes really investable (i.e. no commodities, no bank loans, no private equities);
- different implementation of short selling, in a case with the securities lending and the other with the CFD;
- investment limited only to liquid financial instruments.

It also seems to be common practice, for some asset management companies, that they do not point to perfect replicability for not going to "cannibalize" the corresponding offshore hedge fund's shares.

The database used to conduct the first investigation on the tracking error phenomenon was created from monthly performances, using a single class of investment for each fund and only one currency. The young age of the majority of Newcits funds, and the fact that the corresponding series of offshore hedge funds uses monthly returns, have also permitted the Newcits funds to have only a time series with a very limited length.

5.6 MULTIVARIATE REGRESSION ANALYSIS ON PANEL DATA

Applying the idea that – as with traditional hedge funds (Lhabitant, 2004), – even in the Newcits funds the sources of risk are not different from those of traditional asset classes, we tried to identify risk factors that explain their performance to see if, beyond the ability of managers, there are simply remuneration of new or alternative risks with respect to those identified by the univariate linear regression of the Capital Asset Pricing Model. The results are then compared with those identified by Hasanhodzic and Lo (2006) about the offshore hedge fund industry, in order to quantify the characteristics of minor operational flexibility and improved liquidity of the Newcits fund.

In our analyses, we applied a hedge fund replication model in order to decompose the performance with reference to some key risk factors, according to the specification of Hasanhodzic and Lo (2006). However, as the Newcits phenomenon is mainly European, we felt compelled to identify indices that are more representative of European markets, while Hasanhodzic and Lo (2006) analysed the offshore hedge fund industry using indices of US markets.

We have therefore chosen six risk factors and the following indices to quantify them:

- Currency risk: the Dow Jones Euro Currency Index, which measures the euro exchange rate against G10 currencies.
- Interest rate risk: the AAA government EuroMTS Eurozone total return index, which measures the performance of AAA European government bonds.

- Equity risk: the Stoxx Europe 600 index gross return EUR, containing the prices of the 600 European companies with greatest capitalization.
- Credit risk: the spread between the index Markit iBoxx EUR High Yield Liquid, which contains the 25 most liquid European corporate bonds with a speculative grade type (BB, B and CCC) and the EuroMTS Eurozone government AAA index.
- Commodities risk: the Rogers International Commodity Index Total Return.
- Volatility risk: the implied volatility index Vstoxx of the Euro Stoxx 50.

5.7   EXPOSURE TO RISK FACTORS FOR EACH STRATEGY

Table 5.1 shows the coefficients of the multivariate linear regressions, estimated by the Least Square Dummy Variable model on panel data grouped by investment strategy. Figure 5.12, which is merely a graphical representation of alpha and beta coefficients shown in Table 5.1, enables us to have a clear grasp of the exposure of each strategy to risk factors. For example, the Fixed Income Arbitrage strategy has a significant exposure only to the bond market and not to credit risk, which means that it is taking relative value positions on rates and has no exposure to credit risk.

The analysis is carried out on all euro funds available on Bloomberg's database as of 30 June 2010. Coefficients with a statistical significance lower than 5% are shown in bold type.

5.8   CONTRIBUTION BY FACTOR TO THE HISTORICAL RETURNS

In addition, in order to assess how much of the variance is explained by the model, we have to assess how much of the expected return could be explained at strategy level. The average contribution of each factor to the expected return was initially identified, and the

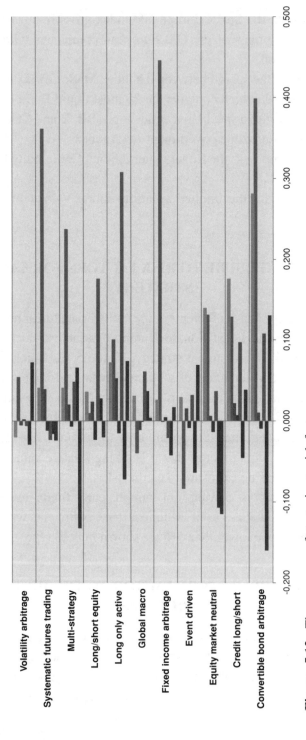

Figure 5.12   The exposure of strategies to risk factors

Table 5.1 Multivariate regression results

Strategy	Sample share	Average Alfa	Beta						Adj. R²
			Eur	Stoxx600	Vstoxx	Cmdty	Irr	Credit	
Convertible bond arbitrage	1%	0.131	**-0.160**	**0.108**	-0.009	0.010	**0.398**	**0.280**	56.9%
Credit long/short	1%	0.038	-0.045	**0.097**	0.007	0.022	0.128	**0.176**	37.7%
Equity market neutral	22%	-0.115	**-0.107**	0.036	**-0.013**	0.006	0.131	**0.139**	3.2%
Event driven	3%	0.069	**-0.063**	**0.032**	**-0.008**	**0.015**	**-0.083**	**0.029**	21.1%
Fixed income arbitrage	6%	0.017	-0.042	-0.021	0.004	0.000	**0.445**	0.026	9.4%
Global macro	9%	0.004	0.037	**0.061**	-0.001	-0.011	-0.039	**0.031**	6.7%
Long only active	4%	0.074	-0.072	**0.307**	**-0.015**	**0.052**	0.100	**0.072**	34.2%
Long/short equity	22%	-0.020	0.027	**0.176**	**-0.023**	0.023	0.009	0.036	13.1%
Multi-strategy	12%	-0.132	**0.066**	**0.048**	**-0.006**	**0.020**	**0.237**	**0.041**	10.1%
Systematic futures trading	12%	-0.024	-0.015	-0.023	**-0.011**	**0.039**	**0.361**	0.041	1.8%
Volatility arbitrage	8%	0.072	-0.029	-0.006	0.002	-0.005	0.054	**-0.019**	3.4%

Note: The coefficients in bold are significantly different from zero at a 5% level or less.

percentage of return was subsequently calculated, as explained by the model.

Through this kind of evaluation, it is possible to:

- identify new or alternative remuneration of risks with respect to the equity risk;
- identify new forms of alternative investment, less costly, more transparent, scalable and liquid products such as the Hedge Fund Replication;
- compare the percentage contributions provided by the factors alpha, beta, and alternative beta (the aggregate of the other five risk factors of the model) in the Newcits industry with respect to the pure hedge fund's industry.

If we consider, for example, the convertible bond arbitrage strategy, from Figure 5.13 you can estimate that more than 50% of the expected returns are explained by the manager ability (in grey) and there is a positive contribution from the equity risk, rate risk and credit risk. Moreover, if we consider the contribution of the operator as part of the performance that the model was unable to locate, and was only indirectly attributed to the operator, we can also quantify how much of each strategy the model can explain of the expected return, and then how much of the expected return of the strategy it would be possible to intercept through a passive management of these six asset classes.

The 31.2% shown by the convertible bond arbitrage strategy in Figure 5.14 is indeed the sum of positive and negative contributions to the expected return of the factors shown above, excluding the manager's contribution. Therefore, when the model is able to explain over 100% of the expected return of a strategy, this means that a passive management of these risk factors would generate a higher ex-post expected return. If we consider, for example, the convertible bond arbitrage strategy, from Figure 5.13 we can estimate that more than 50% of the ex-post expected returns are explained by the manager's ability (shown in grey) and there is a positive contribution from the equity risk, rate risk and credit risk. Moreover, if we consider

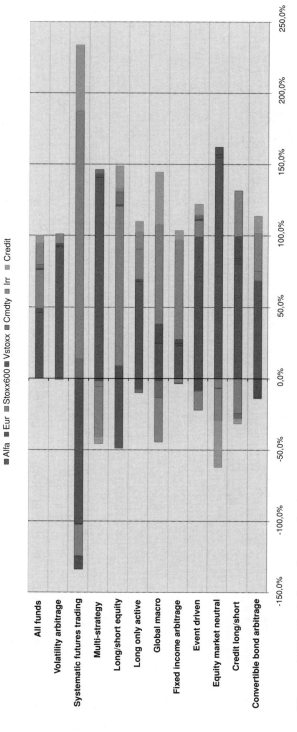

Figure 5.13 Each factor's contribution to expected return

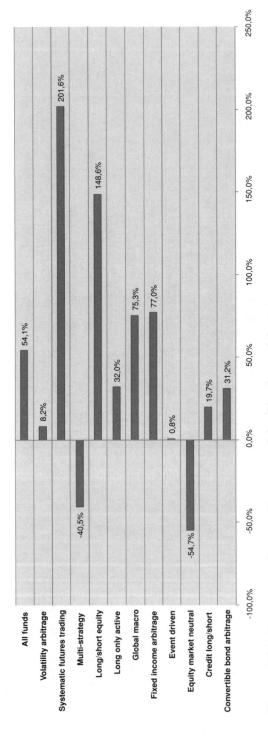

Figure 5.14 Percentage of expected return explained by the model

the contribution of the operator as part of the performance that the model was unable to locate, and was only indirectly attributed to the operator, we can also quantify how much of each strategy the model can explain of the ex-post expected return, and then how much of the ex-post expected return of the strategy would be possible to intercept through a passive management of these six asset classes. The 31.2% shown by the convertible bond arbitrage strategy in Figure 5.14 is indeed the sum of positive and negative contributions to the expected return of the factors shown above, excluding the manager's contribution. Therefore, when the model is able to explain over 100% of the expected return of a strategy, this means that a passive management of these risk factors would generate an higher ex-post expected return.

5.9 LIQUIDITY COMPARISON

Using the autocorrelation coefficient as a proxy for the liquidity of the Newcits funds, we compared the results obtained by Hasanhodzic and Lo (2006) on the offshore hedge fund industry, in order to evaluate the difference in liquidity between the two. Figure 5.15 highlights the higher liquidity of the Newcits funds (shown in grey) consistently for all the strategies compared.

5.10 PERFORMANCE CONTRIBUTION ANALYSIS AT INDUSTRY LEVEL

Finally, we compare the factors that contribute to the expected return (see Figure 5.16). What is clear is the reduction of about 15 percentage points of the alpha factor (or manager's contribution), that could be explained by a reduction of operational flexibility and by the higher liquidity of Newcits funds. In fact, the illiquidity premium of the offshore hedge funds, which is not considered in the multi-factorial model, explains part of the contribution that the alpha generated by offshore hedge funds. So, if we had been explicit about

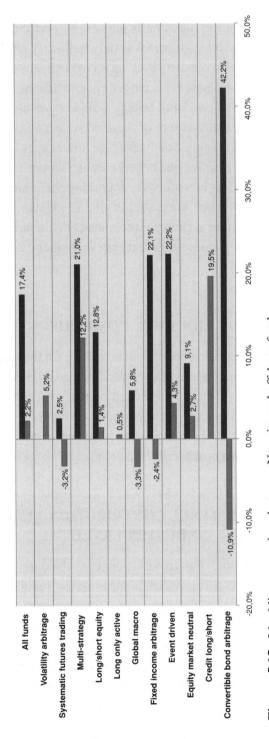

Figure 5.15 Liquidity comparison between Newcits and offshore funds

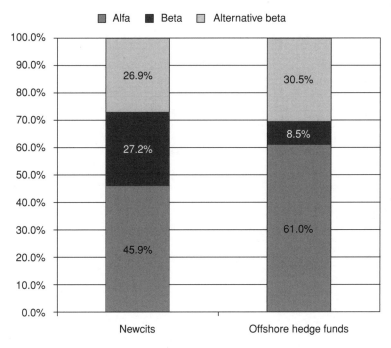

Figure 5.16 Performance contribution at industry level

the illiquidity premium, the alpha generated by offshore hedge funds would have been lower.

While the alternative beta is essentially unchanged, the beta seems to replace the alpha reduction in the Newcits funds. The reason is that the liquidity constraints of Newcits funds require greater exposure to the most liquid asset class, that is equity.

Conclusions

The UCITS III directive paved the way for the convergence between hedge funds and traditional mutual funds.

So far within the UCITS III framework some alternative strategies were available but limited to replicators of hedge fund indices, some global tactical asset allocation products and 130/30 funds[1].

The UCITS III directive provides alternative asset managers a way out of the confidence crisis that hammered the hedge fund industry. It also provides access to retail investors who, in Europe, are not allowed to invest in hedge funds because of the high minimum initial investments and the solicitation ban.

The most relevant innovation of the UCITS III directive passed unnoticed by hedge fund managers until recently: the UCITS III directive allows the use of derivatives for investment and not only for hedging purposes. Many traditional and alternative asset managers have only recently realized that they can implement alternative investment strategies with different risk–return objectives in onshore funds.

So far, the growth of the Newcits industry has been exponential. According to our data as of 30 June 2010, there are 416 Newcits funds and they have raised around €51.8 billion of assets under management (excluding flexible funds, index replicators and global tactical asset allocation products).

---

[1] 130/30 funds are funds with long exposure equal to 130% of fund NAV and short exposure equal to 30% of NAV. This results in a net exposure equal to 100% like a long-only fund, but with the difference that the gross exposure is equal to 160%.

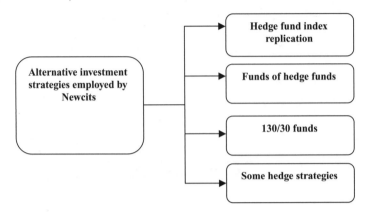

Figure C.1   Alternative investment strategies employed by Newcits

Ease of operation, transparency, asset protection, adequate risk management and standardization are the key success points for Newcits as these characteristics are very appealing for investors. Further, Newcits provide a high level of investor protection towards structural risks; they are also more standardized and provide more transparency and liquidity with respect to offshore hedge funds. As a matter of facts, Newcits give investors access to modified hedge fund strategies, and the investors are not only institutional clients or high net worth individuals, but also potential retail clients. So far, however, this advantage has been more appealing to institutional investors than to retail clients, who are not too familiar with alternative investment strategies.

However, from the perspective of money managers, moral hazard also comes into play in explaining this exceptional growth. At the end of 2009, 78% of hedge funds were under water, and fund managers had a strong incentive to launch fresh funds with a new high watermark. Furthermore, money managers were pushed to launch funds domiciled in Europe by the uncertainty around the new European regulation on offshore hedge funds.

Even if we are at the dawn of this new phenomenon, we can strive to discuss the following potential problems that appear on the horizon:

First, the fee structure is more expensive compared to long-only UCITS III funds: performance fees are around 20%. However, as discussed in Chapter 5, if the most common management fee for an offshore hedge fund is 2%, the average management fee for the retail share class of a Newcits fund is around 1.1%.

The key point is to assess the ability of Newcits to replicate the corresponding offshore hedge fund, where it exists. As a matter of fact, there are asset management companies offering Newcits funds with the aim of replicating offshore hedge funds, and some others that have differentiated the Newcits fund limiting it to a different investable universe – for example, funds limited to different geographical areas with respect to the offshore hedge fund.

In these respects, we analysed the tracking error between the Newcits funds and their corresponding hedge funds offshore. The causes of tracking error are mainly: (1) the different fees and expenses; (2) the implementation of short selling via CFDs rather than via stock borrowing; (3) the higher frequency of subscriptions and redemptions; (4) the different concentration limits and, more generally, the different risk management limits; (5) the ban of investment in commodities, bank loans and private securities; and (6) the fact that, when a new fund is launched, there is a phase of portfolio construction when the gross and net exposures are progressively built.

Another key point is related to the capacity limits of some investment strategies that could soon become a problem with the high inflows entering the Newcits funds.

Moreover, only the most liquid hedge fund strategies can be implemented in Newcits, because they can have at least two redemption dates every month. Therefore the strategies implemented by Newcits have a bias towards large cap equities and futures.

There are also some hidden pitfalls. Liquidity is a financial asset whose price changes over time: this means that when there is a market crisis, some assets that were liquid at the time of investment, could suddenly become illiquid. In these cases, it would not be possible for money managers of Newcits fund to allow redemptions according to ordinary terms. That is why most of the prospectuses of Newcits provide the use of redemption gates.

As far as asset protection is concerned, it is worthwhile to remember that counterparty risk, caused by the use of CFDs, is mitigated by the 20% exposure limit to a single counterparty. However, there is no obligation of daily settlement for the margin of CFDs.

Lastly, we highlighted how some of the limits imposed by the UCITS III are currently circumvented, giving up one of the fundamental pillars of the directive, namely transparency, as in the case of the synthetic Newcits.

Concluding, a final disclaimer is needed. Investors are expected to assess Newcits very carefully before investing, because the UCITS III regulation is broad enough to allow money managers to launch funds that are actually quite complex, and can conceal some potential risk. For these reasons, it is still an open question whether some of these products are suitable for retail investors.

In the medium- to long-term time horizon, we can foresee that liquidity, transparency and a sound risk management will become more and more a *conditio sine qua non* for the success of investment management. In this sense, the UCITS III directive is an opportunity to revitalize the hedge funds industry that, even after the crisis, seem to be capable of generating absolute returns. However, this is going to happen only if the Member State authorities consistently stick to the main pillars of the UCITS regulation.

References

Papers

Beegun, R. and Leroy, P. (2008) Risk management challenges in UCITS III funds. *Journal of Securities Operations & Custody*, **2**(1), 37–52.

CESR (2009) *CESR's Technical Advice at Level 2 on Risk Measurement for the Purposes of the Calculation of UCITS's Global Exposure*.

D'Apice, R. (2009) *Le Principali Novità Introdotte dalla Direttiva UCITS IV e le sue Implicazioni Attuative*. Assogestioni.

Degrada, M. (2009) *Concorrenti o Complementari, è la Strategia che lo Decide*.

Donhoe, J. (2006) *New Strategies for Hedge Funds under UCITS III*. Carne Global Financial Services.

EuroHedge: *Are UCITS Funds the Future in a Hybrid Asset Management World?*

FEFSI (2002) *The New UCITS Directive Explained*.

Gentili, M.P. (2005) *Disciplina e Fiscalità delle SICAV Lussemburghesi e Italiane*.

Hauser, J. and Petit, M. (2008) Examining alternative strategies within the context of UCITS III regulations. *Journal of Securities Law, Regulation & Compliance*, **2**(1), 19–28.

O'Callaghan, A. and McManus, D. (2009) Risk management in UCITS III funds. *Journal of Securities Law, Regulation & Compliance*, **2**(2), 115–124.

Books

Hasanhodzic, J. and Lo, A.W. (2006) Can Hedge-Fund Returns be Replicated?: The Linear Case (August 16, 2006). Available at SSRN: http://ssrn.com/abstract=924565.

Jorion, P. (2007) *Financial Risk Manager Handbook.* John Wiley & Sons Inc.

Lhabitant, F. (2004) *Hedge Funds: Quantitative Insights.* John Wiley & Sons Ltd.

Stefanini, F. (2005) *Hedge Funds, Strategie di Investimento.* Il Sole 24 Ore.

Stefanini, F. (2006) *Investment Strategies of Hedge Funds.* John Wiley & Sons Ltd.

Regulation

CSSF Circular 07/308.

Direttiva 85/611 CE del Parlamento Europeo e del Consiglio.

Direttiva 2001/107/CE del Parlamento Europeo e del Consiglio (Management Company Directive).

Direttiva 2001/108/CE del Parlamento Europeo e del Consiglio (Product Directive).

Direttiva 2007/16/CE del Parlamento Europeo e del Consiglio (Clarification Directive).

Websites

www.aima.org

www.assogestioni.it/index.cfm/1,652,0,49,html/la-direttiva-ucits-iv

www.borsaitaliana.it/documenti/rubriche/sottolalente/cfd-contracts-for-difference.htm

www.dexia-am.com/

www.efama.org

Acronyms

AUM	Assets under management
CAGR	Compound annual growth rate
CESR	Committee of European Securities Regulators
CFD	Contract for difference
CSSF	Commission de Surveillance du Secteur Financier
CTA	Commodity trading advisor
FAS	Financial accounting standards
FCP	Fonds communs de placement
ISD	Investment service directive
KID	Key investor document
KII	Key investor information
MBS	Mortgage-backed securities
NAV	Net asset value
OECD	Organization for Economic Co-operation and Development
OEIC	Open-ended investment company
OTC	Over-the-counter
RMP	Risk management process
SEC	Securities and Exchange Commission
SICAV	Société d'Investissement a Capital Variable
UCITS	Undertaking for collective investment in transferable securities
VAR	Value at risk

Index